THE ARTISTRY OF GLORIA NAYLOR AS REFLECTED IN HER SELECT NOVELS

DR. P. K. SELVARAJ & DR. K. RAJKUMAR

Copyright © Dr. P. K. Selvaraj & Dr. K. Rajkumar
All Rights Reserved.

ISBN 979-888591181-8

Dedication

To the Almighty

Contents

About The Authors

Dr. P. K. Selvaraj is working as Assistant Professor of English in College of Business and Social Sciences, Asmara University, North East Africa. He has done M.A., M.Ed., MPhil.,MBA(HR) and Ph.D. in English Literature. He has 5 years of college teaching experience in India and 7 years of University college teaching experience abroad. He has participated in various workshops/seminars/conferences. He has over 5 years of research experience and published four articles in International journals.

He has strong belief in self-motivation, an impulse for excellence and the feeling of independence has helped him in updating his knowledge anddesigned reorientation of the subject matter. He has extensive hands on experience in conceptualizing strategies, building and binding confidence level and measuring the performance of young learners.

Dr. K. Rajkumar is working as Assistant Professor of English at Nehru Arts and Science College (Autonomous), Coimbatore. He has done post-graduation in both English and Linguistics. He holds M.Phil. and Ph.D. degrees in English. He has a total of 9 years of college teaching experience. His area of specialization is Language and Literature. He has over 6 years of research experience. He has authored one book and published more than 15 articles in National and International journals, he has also visited and presented paper in International Conference abroad.

Preface

This book deals with the Artistry of the well known African-American modern woman novelist namely Gloria Naylor. Her first novel *The Women of Brewster Place* which was awarded as Best First Novel for American Book Award of1982. Gloria Naylor ranks among writers like William Faulkner who popularized social issues including slavery that many American writers may not prefer to talk about. Naylor was very unapologetic in writing about racial and class discrimination, gender issues, racism, modernism, naturalism, sexuality and urbanization. Through her characters she showed how a black person could recreate real life images and stories.

Artistry is the act of turning new and creative ideas into reality. It is characterized by the ability to perceive the world in new dimensions, to unlock hidden patterns, to make associations between apparently unrelated phenomena, and to produce solutions. Naylor's themes of wish, survival and individual redemption, articulated in a series of novels and essays, won her popular applause. All her novels are linked together by mentioning the characters and places in individual stories. Naylor's novel explores the issues related to racism and sexism which are clearly marked in her writings.

This book is an evidence of the artistry in her works as exemplified from the novels, *The Women of Brewster Place, Linden Hills* and *Mama Day*. The depiction of characters, plots, themes, symbolism, sexism, racism, naturalism, modernism and postmodernism are a few of her striking features. The objective is to prove her artistic excellence that surrounds her personality despite the trauma she might have felt of the ethnic discrimination and failure to be recognized as a mainstream writer. With the help of contemporary and historical approach, this book attempts to highlight the struggles and anxieties of Gloria Naylor and how she rose to be an important woman African American writer in the post-colonial era.

CHAPTER ONE

Introduction

Gloria Naylor wrote novels that emphasized the strengths of women and men particularly African-American men, women and the possessions on their lives due to racism, sexism and survival. She concentrated on the black community, instead of analyzing the effects of discrimination on black people. The consideration of black women was trivialized and distorted by the white gender's perspective and in the majority of her novels Naylor seemed intent upon representing, re-visioning and quite purely expressing the several perspectives of black women. Artistry is the process of bringing something new into being. Artistry requires passion and dedication. It brings to our consciousness what was formerly hidden and points to new life. Artistry involves two processes thinking and producing. The artistic work of African American women writers can also be said to form a motivation ever since Phillis Wheatley (1753-1784) wrote her first piece of poetry *On being brought from Africa to America* eventually showing that she wrote that slavery was a "cruel fate." From that time, novelists, dramatists and poets have been bestowing their pieces from a vibrant field of colors and textures. They have drawn their encouragement from the women before them and around them, and from their own secret and suppressed fears and fancies, hopes and dreams.

Gloria Naylor: Her Life and Works

Gloria Naylor was born in Harlem (New York City) on January 25, 1950, and the eldest child of Alberta McAlpin Naylor and

Roosevelt Naylor who migrated north to New York City shortly before Gloria's birth. Her passion for reading was nurtured by her mother, who remembered her personal experiences with her native Mississippi's segregated public libraries. Unable to borrow books, Alberta Naylor had been enforced to earn money to buy them, so she encouraged Gloria and her two sisters (Fanny Bernice and Carolyn) to visit the libraries in New York once they were old enough to write their names on their library cards. Her quest for reading and love of libraries is also greatly inherited by her from her mother. Her parents gave her the lessons of self-validation, independence and self-confidence. She became a keen reader and began to write poems and stories as a child. Naylor's mother encouraged her to read and gave her a journal to write down her thoughts and took this advice to her mind.

This transformed her personality to a great extent. Becoming the missionary of Jehovah's Witness brought her out of her shyness and gave her a basis, a community and a chance to travel. They even encouraged her unique and magnificent power of imagination and clearly believed in her power of written word which truly worked wonders for Naylor in future. Though this missionary work brought her out of shy envelop and also pushed her softly into travel and meeting people, it also fascinated her in a different world of hermits. This was a literary setback for her since she was unaware of the explosion of the black literature that was exploding around her. This also segregated her, to a point, from her own culture as she did not recognize the unbelievable rising of the Black literature. These shaped her personality as an individual as well as a writer.

She spent her years in the propagation of the message from 1968 to 1975, as the missionary of the Jehovah witness, in New York and around Dunn, North Carolina, in Jacksonville, Florida and also preached as a pioneer for the Jehovah's Witnesses. She traveled all over the country. In this time span of seven years, she supported herself as a switchboard operator. She left the Jehovah's missionary and had a nervous breakdown when she moved back to her parent's home. Then she took up to the work of a switchboard operator as a full time job. She did this from 1975 to 1981 and also got enrolled in Medgar Evers College to seek a degree in nursing. But most of her time was now being engaged by the study of literature and therefore transferred to the Brooklyn College of the City University of New York. It was here in this place that she realized her importance as a Woman and a Black American. She realized the awakening of her identity when she was introduced to the great black women writers here. This added energy to her passion and fascination to write her own books. As a passionate reader from childhood, she already admired writers as Dickens, the Brontes, Faulkner, Ellison and Baldwin. It is essential to note that she still had never read a novel by a black woman at that time. Deeply influenced by Toni Morrison's novel *The Bluest Eye* (1970), Naylor made her own venture into writing in 1979 when she submitted her first short story, *A Life on Beekman Place* to *Essence* magazine, and was encouraged by the magazine and received a publishing contract for her first novel *The Women of Brewster Place* (1982).

According to Naylor, family and group of people portray her communal history as a black American. One of the excerpts of an interview:

Angels Carabi: I would like to talk about your books now. From the very beginning you create a sense of place, a sense of community where people interact.

Gloria Naylor: Yes, that's right. You know, you're asking good questions and it is not easy to answer them quickly....

Besides, there is my communal history as a black American. Our survival today has depended upon our nurturing each other, finding our resources from within ourselves.

That sense of self-determination, taking care of your own is in my racial blood, meaning just my whole history. It's in my personal life because of the type of family. I had and the class of people that I grew up around with.

I think that all those factors explain why I tend to work with communities.

-- An interview with Angels Carabi in 1992.

Naylor explained her writing methods to Essence in 1995: "I tell the essence of a story not so much through my characters' words as by capturing a moment in time, frozen and perfect, when all their senses create a living reality." She expanded on her philosophy in Essence three years later.

"Artists should be able to write about whatever they want," she said. "There's a lot of self-censorship in our community, which is a shame. People feel that they need to write role models, not just good characters."

In a conversation with Toni Morrison she commented:

I wrote because I had no choice, but that was a long road from gathering the authority within myself to believe that I could actually be a writer. The writers I had been taught to love were either male or white. And who was I to argue that Ellison, Austen, Dickens, the Brontes, Baldwin and

Faulkner weren't masters? They were and are. But inside there was still the faintest whisper. Was there no one telling my story? And since it appeared there was not how could I presume to? . . . [Reading] The Bluest Eye [was] the beginning [of the ability to conceive myself as a writer] . . . The presence of the work . . . said to a young black woman, struggling to find a mirror of her worth in this society, not only is your story worth telling but it can be told in words so painfully eloquent that it becomes a song. --- A Conversation with Toni Morrison.

She won the American Book Award for Best First Novel, as well as the Distinguished Writer Award from the Mid-Atlantic Writers Association for this novel. In 1983 Naylor received a master's degree from Yale University in African American Studies, where her second novel, *Linden Hills* (1985), became her master's thesis. As well, she became a writer-in-residence at Cummington Community of the Arts and a visiting lecturer at George Washington University.

Naylor uses different quads to tell the stories of Afro-American women. Usually, the location of setting of the characters continue in her forthcoming novel and this connection helps the reader to establish a history, a society and a useful sense of stability in a place where a story, however original, can be told and believed. In these years, Naylor witnessed a distinct transformation in her own life and found a new scope in her as a Black woman. She even discovered facts about feminism and got revitalized with the African-American literature. A number of factors contributed to Gloria Naylor's developing social, political awareness, environment, well-known background, community and African-American tradition, her educational background and her early life's knowledge.

The Women of Brewster Place

She is ideal in the creation of the corrupt fictional worlds in which characters must find some sort of a sanctuary to be safe. *The Women of Brewster Place* takes up from Richard Wright's *Native Son* and Ann Petry's *The Street*. In its representation of the effects of city lifestyles and incorporates the influence of Shakespeare, "engaging European as well as American traditions." Naylor associates the clamp of the late twentieth century with the deadly sins of old, representing the economic affluence and the culture of individuality of urban culture had positively fostered the influences of love, envy, greediness and betrayal on human life. Naylor's use of character imagery or her creation of well-meaning male characters is not mentioned in this sensitive piece of the artistic study. It talks about absent fathers, aggressive husbands and running away sons, but it remains still about the presence of Ben (a character in *TWBP*) who expresses his readiness to allow the lesbian couple in the community of the block and goes out of his way to be of some help to the worried women of this community. However, she has written a complete novel comprised of the affirmation and bonding of these seven women who were frightened together in close relationship to one another when they all ended up on Brewster Place. Female bonding and emotional sympathy are presented in the women are the patterns along which the seven chapters of *The Women of Brewster Place* are joined together.

Brewster Place was first spirituallycleaned with sparkling wine, and then with blood and vomit. The baptisms strongly represent the vast gap between the promised and the unfulfilled American dream. Naylor's novel is about women managing in the men's world, and in the white humanity.

Linden Hills

The central theme of her second novel *Linden Hills* (LH) is mainly resistance and rebirth. Naylor has made the position that attempting to mount in the ranks of white-dominated society through economic means, outcome in a shallow victory. The first idea for this novel was inclined by her reading of *The Inferno* in a Great Literature course. *Linden Hills* is an African- American middle-class neighborhood elegant after the encircling geography of Dante's *Hell*. Two younger poets, outsiders in Linden Hills who are looking for employment the week previous to Christmas, find out the obsession and crime of the middle class residents, who have abandon culture and standards for material gain.

Linden Hills is the novel of a Black woman's expedition towards granting of political, social or economical power to an individual or group. This expedition gives her the self-belief and results in self-actualization. Naylor in *Linden Hills* investigates gender relations along with discrimination to examine into African-American uniqueness. By contrast, *Linden Hills* narrates the effects of a place where human value undergoes a complicated evaluation and a firm separation from the white middle class. Naylor uses the formation of Dante's *Inferno* to describe a middle-class society preoccupied with material gain. A set of laws of Linden Hills are made by a man. The women in this place do not have names, in truth, the most important female character is only known as "Luther's wife" until nearly the end of the novel. Naylor's novel is not only an assessment of avarice but also a feminist story of women's unspoken history, as Willa, banished to the vault for producing a light-skinned son, garners power from the sandy testimonies of her predecessors. A world of triumphant Black Americans is portrayed in this novel. These Black Americans however have obtained a status along to lead their livelihood but in turn they have to surrender their hearts and souls though they are perfect in their workplace.

Mama Day

Mama Day (MD) was Naylor's third and first unchaptered novel. In *Mama Day*, Naylor has combined her desired characters and personality, creating George, the eventual gentleman and lover, Miranda Day, the wisest of conjure women, Cocoa, playful but sound, the young, modern black woman. Naylor develops the idea of spirituality in *Mama Day*, which explores the work of art as individual faith. The women in this novel live on a distant island called Willow Springs, where the remedial powers of Miranda Day and her ancestors are entirely accepted by the island's residents. Willow Springs also provides a breathing space where these women are quite distant from any white dominant culture. It is set in two different worlds which are associated by a wooden bridge. Naylor's imagination of all black community, located on a peaceful island of Willow Springs, existing and prosperous at the same time with an actual mixture of races, modern day New York City has made *Mama Day* a greatly perused novel among Naylor's works.

The story of *Mama Day* develops with important changes. It departs from the world of real situation and fit in myth and magic which becomes the essence of the novel. About her way of writing, different writers have different range of vision that Naylor presents a fresh picture of relationships among women, of female friendship, sisterhood, and community. Naylor's rewriting of the sixteenth century works of English rebirth, particularly those of Shakespeare, in her first three novels. Naylor is a talented author at giving world literature an African-American spin. Her works undoubtedly craft the fact- *Mama Day* of Naylor lends a lot from *The Tempest* by William Shakespeare. In this novel, Naylor combines her Southern surroundings with her Northern environment, expressing her warm appreciation of the African American woman and her bias towards the African American man, blending magic and myth with ordinary realism. There is a lot in *Mama Day* which perches on the border of faith, and this is what imparts a noticeably African aroma to a tale placed in America.

Bailey's Cafe

The fourth novel *Bailey's Café* (BF) is an attractive creation and at many places feels like the *Canterbury Tales.* In Chaucer's Canterbury Tales Harry Bailey was the host at Tabard Inn and the similarity can be obviously seen with the narrators of Naylor's *Bailey's Café.* The characters recite themselves their stories of devastated hopes and deteriorated imaginings. *Bailey's Cafe* is about a man, who runs a Brooklyn cafe frequented by an all black cast of characters, including Eve (brothel owner), Sadie (prostitute), Miss Maple (a heterosexual cross-dresser), Jesse Bell (lesbian) and Bailey himself, who provides asylum to these characters, who tell him their life stories. Naylor's sensitive narrative and gift for characterization have been compared with Sherwood Anderson's classic, *Wines burg, Ohio.* Each and every fictional character of this novel has a horrible background and being socially and politically exploited, they finally try to live their lives with their own convenience. Though these characters in the novel are professionally harlots but primarily they are not prostitutes. While in the external world these characters may be thought of as misfits, in the cafe, each one achieves a transcendent status and serves as a symbol of the triumph of perseverance over adversity. Once again, Naylor demonstrated her ability to show the non-violence protest in the lives of the common people.

The narration is done by the cafe's cook and manager. The structure of the story is lyrical. This lyrical language gives the effect of no less than jazz and blues. The songs mentioned are sung by the characters themselves and in turn empower them to generate the hope for a living. Naylor establishes an atmosphere for all Afro-American women to reveal their thoughts, emotional states, and consciousness and be in the search for a solution for their difficulties and complications. The Cafe not only emerges as the setting of the whole story, but creates a free of oppression place for all the Afro-American women who take shelter to Cafe. Naylor in this novel skillfully discusses the effects of gender relations and racism on Black identity. She displays her intimate knowledge of the Biblical tales and verses. In this instance, Naylor uses the Bible more effectively than she had used *The Inferno* to enrich and support her work. *Bailey's Cafe* is an exercise in retelling andrecreating stories of women, rescuing these biblical tales from the distortions of patriarchal influences and recasting them into the mould of the lives of modern day women.

The Men of Brewster Place

In 1998, Naylor's artistic view falls on Brewster Place, thus focusing on the male residents, in *The Men of Brewster Place* (TMBP). The novel is clearly a reply and even a continuation to *The Women of Brewster Place.* It may even be a follow-up to *Mama Day.* Naylor's writing is stirring in advance as if it is written in an unpredictable style. The style itself finish the analysis of the structure of an artistic work. Her victory as a writer transcends both her cultural identity and gender. She is the most important Afro-American woman novelist, most notable, and a most noteworthy and significant writer on the literary scenario. In this novel *The Men of Brewster Place,* Naylor adds to her portraits of women living in a town shelter project in The Women of Brewster Place, an arcade of male profiles. Naylor turns her interest towards the difficulty of the black men who are in dilemma and immediately want to apologize in front of their female partners. Each and every character in the novel whether married or non-married, is attached with a female with odd relation, commits his fault and wants to live with them being a friend, lover, husband and father. All these characters are generally insecure and politically weak to face any problems, to resume their normal life with unity. According to *The African American Review,* it a much required glimpse into the personal life of black men from a black woman's perception. *The African-American Review* noted the lyrical prose which readers have come to expect from the talented novelist and that the male characters lack a lot of emotional attachment and depth that make Naylor's female characters more memorable.

Literary Legacy

In the literary arena of African American writings, Gloria Naylor stands as an example of contemporary writers of fiction because she herself is a part of all that she writes.

Her novels are often inspired by her appreciation of literary masters like William Shakespeare, Dante and Toni Morrison. Naylor's great artistic senses of decorating her novels are unique. She linked her first story with the second novel is an example of her uniqueness. She normally uses the devices to create a sane connection from the story of one novel to the other. The best example can be taken from *Mama Day*, which is her third novel gives the beginning of George at *Bailey's Cafe* (fourth novel). Another example can be cited of *Linden Hills* which is a version of Dante's *Inferno* and in the similar style like *Mama Day* has the influence of *The Tempest* by William Shakespeare and Toni Morrison's *Song of Solomon*.

In the recent times, Naylor has earned a name which is associated with critical and commercial success. She is appreciated in academic circles and recognized in the world of literary society. She is rightly acknowledged for speaking out the rights of women and other communal issues. Critics have paid less attention to Naylor's representation of race politics in *The Women of Brewster Place* and have honored Naylor's exploration of feminist concerns in her representation of the strengths of black sisterhood and her use of dream pattern. Some of the critics have grounded the female powers of Sapphira Wade and Mama Day in their interweaving analysis of words. Adriane L. Ivey makes an excellent attempt to read Naylor's two novels, namely *Bailey's Cafe* and *Mama Day*, as a rewriting of the most religious or applicable text of the Western culture.

Understanding Gloria Naylor by Margret Earley Whitt is one of the complete attempts that have been made by critics to evaluate Naylor's vision. The noteworthy study is to analyze Naylor's artistic skills in relating literary texts (intertextuality) in terms of her shrewd use of Shakespeare, Dante, the Bible, Walt Whitman, T. S. Eliot, existing Afro-American writers and the world of ballet and sadness in the portrayal of her characters, plots and imagery. Margret Earley Whitt has laid a special emphasis on how Naylor's characters are interconnected with the places they dwell in and how their interconnections are armored when they re-occur in Naylor's successive novels. But, her study is in a frail position by her method of organization. Her study is based on the character. So each and every major character is selected and analyzed under the experience and maturity. Likewise, the characters have been discussed based on their respective novels.

Naylor has won a National Endowment for the Arts fellowship in 1985 and also served as a Cultural Exchange Lecturer in India for United States Information Agency for three weeks. She was a visiting professor at New York University in 1986. In *New York Times* she wrote several *HERS* columns on topics such as psychics, dating and the popularity of the television game show *Wheel of Fortunate*. She even won the Candace Award of the National Coalition of One Hundred Black Women. In *Reflections*, a piece in *Centennial*, she interviewed her parents, in their thirty sixth year of marriage, about their jagged reasons for coming to New York and parting the South.

The subsequent chapters will bring out the artistry and spot Naylor's artistic explanation and the issues she struggles with as a writer, feminist, and an African American woman of this era. This book undertakes to examine Gloria Naylor's offerings and persistence of the African American literary custom. Naylor's writings are placed side by side especially with other associated texts, namely the writings of her predecessors and contemporaries. Such comparisons serve to contextualize Naylor's work, and more, to highlight the literary words (intertextuality) within it, an intertextuality which heretofore had not been possibly given the narrow accessibility of literary works by African American women writers before the 1970s. Naylor's works are discussed in this proposal are the issues of socio-economic defeat of women, women bonding, women's sexuality, the language of women, and the adjustment of female characters in the novels. Naylor is a part of the

African American literary custom, particularly that of its women writers.

Chapterization

The current research has six chapters. Chapter one is introduction. It provides the history of the African Novel with a brief life history of Naylor, her place in literary legacy of Afro-American writers followed by a detailed account of each novel. It also sketches the literary legacy of the author and gives the scope of the book.

Chapter two entitled, "Historical Background of Contemporary African American Literature" deals with an overall view of contemporary African American literature by unfolding the background of the historical events that noticed its development. This chapter focuses on Early Challenges and Black Narratives, Slave Narratives, Black Arts Movement, Multiculturalism, African American Literature, Era of Reconstruction, Harlem Renaissance, Protest Era, Literary Naturalism, Modernism, Post Modernism and famous African American writers of the time. In the 1970s women began to honestly express their experience as both suppressed women and portions of marginal groups. The black women writers of the period – Gloria Naylor, Toni Cade Bambara, Shirley Anne Williams, and Gayl Jones – explored the issues of their challenging situation and struggle for emancipation in a racial and conservative culture. Their work made a significant change in African-American literature. At last, this chapter also deals with Literature review of previous researches of Gloria Naylor's novels.

Chapter three entitled, "*The Women of Brewster Place*: The Search for a Home or Blending of Lives" interrogates the artistic skills of Gloria Naylor, in her first novel. The chapter contains introduction, artistic characters of the novel, plot – the failure of American dream, themes – fractured relationships, symbolism - Communal harmony and conclusion. It discusses the creative characters how they highlight the social and political condition of the Afro-Americans. Through her plot and theme, she proves herself as a "wordsmith" which means storyteller. She introduced the readers the seven female characters and their fractured relationship, who for their social grade, liberty, equality, economic and political development face and experience sensitive suffering and anguish. After facing enough unkindness as well as exploitation they come out in order to close to the ruling group. According to Naylor, symbolically these are the stories of the hopes, despairs, lust and caring of the women of Brewster Place. Till the end, they remain women capable of love and trust and this love and trust is also the core foundation of their problems, miseries and despairs.

Chapter four entitled *"Linden Hills:* Chauvinistic Relations and Reflection on Female Black Identity" is a critique of Gloria Naylor's second novel, *Linden Hills* which examines the imaginary Black women characters expedition towards granting of political, social or economical power to an individual or group. This expedition resembles the infernal bough and gives her the self-belief and results in self-actualization. This chapter contains introduction, artistic characters of the novel, plot – the infernal bough, themes – postcolonial legacy, symbolism - an allegorical narrative and conclusion. Naylor in *Linden Hills* investigates gender relations along with discrimination to examine into African-American uniqueness. By contrast, *Linden Hills* narrates the effects of a place where human value undergoes a complicated evaluation to and firm separation from the white middle class. As the theme, Postcolonial inheritance is applied in this novel by Naylor in the formation of Dante's Inferno to describe a middle-class society preoccupied with material gain. Naylor used the allegorical narrative style to represent symbolism in this novel. Naylor's novel is not only an assessment of avarice but also a feminist story of women's unspoken history. A world of triumphant Black Americans is portrayed in this novel. These Black Americans however have obtained a status along to lead their livelihood but in turn they have to surrender their hearts and souls though they are perfect in their workplace.

Chapter five entitled *"Mama Day:* Exploring the Spirituality" is an analysis of Naylor's third and first unchaptered novel. This chapter focuses on the following subtitles- introduction, artistic characters of the novel, plot – human relationships, themes – the emotional motherhood, symbolism – the ancestral inheritance and conclusion. In *Mama Day*, Naylor has combined her creative characters and personality, creating George, the eventual gentleman and lover, Miranda Day, the wisest of conjure women, Cocoa, playful but sound, the young, modern black woman. Naylor develops the idea of spirituality in *Mama Day*, which explores the work of art as human relationships and individual faith.

Chapter six is the conclusion of this study. This chapter is a summing up of the previous chapters and findings of this study. Based on the discussions and analyses, this chapter highlights how Naylor sued her great artistic sense of decorating her novels. She connected her first story with the second novel is an instance of her individuality as a contemporary writer. She normally uses the devices to create a sane connection from the story of one novel to the other.

Historical Background of Contemporary Afro – American Literature

Introduction

Afro - American literary history begins with the study of the history and the origin of African American art, music, and literature. This literature is the complete series of literary works by the immigrants of African origin from Africa to United States of America. Before knowing the Background of Afro – American Literature it is essential to know about the problems of race and attraction of coloured Africans of that period to write. The history of African – American people is spotted with bondage which is portrayed by incessant humiliation, racial discrimination, dehumanization and exploitation. Slave narratives expose the historical background of America at the time of slavery. For decades together Americans and Europeans with racial notions of lowliness recognized Afro – Americans to the inferior species and ignored their ethic, culture and linguistic standards. These people were remarked as people with no history, no traditional inheritance, no custom, and no identity in America. Those negative descriptions were created by English travellers and merchants who visited the African Continent.

In this chapter, the reader will be provided with a historical background right from the early times of slave narratives to the rise of the Black Literature, African American Literature, the advent of era of reconstruction, Harlem Renaissance and the modern contemporary period.

Early Challenges and Black Narratives

Early in the 18th century, laws excluded the testimony of the black in court especially in the South. In several colonies, the free black paid punitive taxation and were prohibited from owning property. Some blacks lost the right to vote in Virginia. They were brought against their willingness and many wives were separated from their husbands and were given to others. Kenneth Warren states that, African Americans were given different names like 'Negros' 'Black' 'Coloured' and 'Afro - American'. These Afro - Americans were denied of fundamental rights like to read and to write. As a result, the appearance of the novel writing custom became a highly natured challenge.

The Slave Narratives

The Afro - American literature from the period of the slave narratives to till date has become a part deeply embedded with thoughts about culture which characterizes human anxieties. Suppressing the Black community from their economic and communal rights roused the black individuals to react and retort. These social and historical events pushed many African Americans to be poets and writers because they want to get social justice and freedom.

The slave narratives were the outcome of the clashes between the Whites who supported slavery from southern part of America and the northern slaves who were seeking freedom from the harassment of slavery, so black people use the writing as a tool for the better place in the society. They named themselves as Afro – Americans or Black Americans, at present known with a concrete name of their own as African – Americans. A close analysis of African – American literature from slave narratives to the present writings of Black writers was the main focus in this study. The literature read at that time in England presented a negative interpretation of Africans and their ways of life. The Africans were labelled as ruthless and dreadful people. For the past three hundred years of incessant struggle and isolation of the African American's under the Western's initiated support for their society through the fictional works called slave narratives. Slave narratives were the beginning of Afro – American literature. Most of the writings at the time of slavery were autobiographical.

The main objective of this chapter is to portray a clear picture of background of the Black Literature, and how it proved a milestone for American Literature. Some of the masterworks of American literature were produced by the direct effects of the slave narratives, Mark Twain's *Huckleberry Finn* and Stowe's *Uncle Tom's Cabin*, and the award winning novels of Styron's *The Confession of Nat Turner* and Toni Morrison's *Beloved*, show the direct effects of the slave narratives. Andrews Williams states the success of the Afro – American writers in his *Towards a Poetics of Afro – American Autobiography* as, "a salutary effect on the black community's sense of its own literary resources and on the literate community's sense of the importance of those resources."

Black Arts Movement

The Black Arts Movement often called Black Aesthetics Movement (BAM) is the artistic outgrowth of the Black Power movement that was prominent in the 1960s and early 1970s. The people involved in the Black Arts Movement used the arts as a way to free themselves. The movement served as a catalyst for many different ideas and cultures to come alive. This was a chance for African Americans to express themselves in a way that most would not have expected. Time magazine describes the Black Arts Movement as the "single most controversial movement in the history of African-American literature" – possibly in American literature as a whole. The movement has been seen as one of the most important times in African-American literature. It inspired black people to establish their own publishing houses, magazines, journals and art institutions. It led to the creation of African-American Studies programs within universities.

It also describes a set of attitudes about African-American cultural production, which assumed that political activism was a primary responsibility of black artists. It also decreed that the only valid political end of black artists' efforts was liberation from white political and artistic power structures. Just as white people were to be stripped of their right to proscribe or define black identity, white aesthetic standards was to be overthrown and replaced with creative values arising from the black community. The Black artist takes this to mean that his primary duty is to speak to the spiritual and cultural needs of Black people. Therefore, the main thrust of this new class of contemporary writers is to challenge the contradictions arising out of the Black man's experience in the racist West. Currently, these writers are re-evaluating western aesthetics, the traditional role of the writer, and the social function of art. Implicit in this re-evaluation is the need to develop a "black aesthetic." Consequently, the Black Arts Movement is an ethical movement. Ethical, that is, from the viewpoint of the oppressed. And much of the oppression confronting the Third World and Black America is directly traceable to the Euro American cultural sensibility. This sensibility, anti-human in nature, has, until recently, dominated the psyches of most Black artists and intellectuals; it must be destroyed before the Black creative artist can have a meaningful role in the transformation of society.

The effects of this movement are as follows:

African Americans became a greater presence not only in the field of literature but in all areas of the arts. Theater groups, poetry performances, music and dance were central to the movement.

- It allowed African Americans the chance to express their voices in the mass media as well as become involved in communities.

- The Black Arts Movement also provided incentives for public funding of the arts and increased public support of various arts initiatives.

- The struggle for freedom—social, psychological, and aesthetic—is the distinguishing attribute of African American literature.

The movement lasted for about a decade, through the mid-1960s and into the 1970s. The following features of BAM can be summed as under

a. First, it was a period of controversy and change in the world of literature.
b. It brought the portrayal of new ethnic voices in the United States.
c. English-language literature, prior to the Black Arts Movement, was dominated by white authors.
d. African Americans became a greater presence not only in the field of literature but in all areas of the arts.
e. Theater groups, poetry performances, music and dance were central to the movement.
f. Through different forms of media, African Americans were able to educate others about the expression of cultural differences and viewpoints.
g. Last but not the least black fiction of the African Americans used vernacular dialects.

These features were mostly reflected in the activities of Harlem Writers Guild, a group of Black Americans. The group included black writers such as Maya Angelou and Rosa Guy. This group often used political slogans to express its ideas. Theater performances were also used to convey community issues and organizations. The theaters, as well as cultural centers, were based throughout America and were used for community meetings, study groups and film screenings. Newspapers were a major tool in spreading the Black Arts Movement. In 1964, Black Dialogue was published, making it the first major Arts movement publication.

The Black Arts Movement, although short, is essential to the history of the United States. It spurred political activism and use of speech throughout every African American community. It allowed African Americans the chance to express their voices in the mass media as well as become involved in communities

Relationship between Multiculturalism and BAM

There would be no multiculturalism movement without Black Arts. Latinos, Asian Americans, and others all say they began writing as a result of the example of the 1960s. Blacks gave the example that you don't have to assimilate. You could do your own thing; get into your own background, your own history, your own tradition and your own culture. The Blacks set the challenge for cultural sovereignty. Theatre groups, poetry performances, music and dance were centered on this movement, and therefore African Americans gained social and historical recognition in the area of literature and arts. According to the Academy of American poets, many writers- Native Americans, Latinos, gays and lesbians, and younger generations of African Americans have acknowledged their debt to the Black Arts Movement. The BAM also granted a political voice to black artists (including poets, dramatists, writers, musicians, etc.).

This research study aims to discuss Gloria Naylor's notions of marginalized Identities in her novels with regard to Black American themes that were prevalent during this period.

It can be argued that the Black Arts movement produced some of the most exciting novels, drama, dance, music and visual art and that many important "post-Black artists" such as Toni Morrison, Ntozake Shange, Alice Walker, and August Wilson were shaped by the movement. Among the well-known writers who were involved with the movement are Nikki Giovanni, Sonia Sanchez, Maya Angelou, Hoyt W. Fuller, and Rosa Guy. Although not strictly part of the Movement, other notable African-American writers such as novelists Toni Morrison and Ishmael Reed share some of its artistic and thematic concerns. Although Reed is neither a movement apologist nor advocate, he said: "I think what Black Arts did was inspiring a whole lot of Black people to write."

As mentioned earlier, the Harlem Writers Guild, led by John O. Killens, which included Maya Angelou, Jean Carey Bond, Rosa Guy, and Sarah Wright among others, contributed largely to production of Afro American literature. Black Arts Movement granted a political voice to black artists (including novelists, poets, dramatists, writers, musicians, etc.). For instance, Amiri Baraka's "Black Art (poem)" serves as one of his most controversial, yet poetically profound supplements to the Black Arts Movement.

In this piece, Baraka merges politics with art, criticizing poems that are not useful or adequately representative of the Black struggle. First published in 1966, a period particularly known for the Civil Rights Movement, the political aspect of this piece underscores the need for a concrete and artistic approach to the realistic nature involving racism and injustice.

Amiri Baraka also wrote an essay entitled "The Revolutionary Theatre" that serves as an important contribution to the Black Arts Movement. This Essay shows how the Black Arts Movement involved the progression of blacks in the art world, which includes theatre and explains. It imposes that the world is not ready for a change but that it must change in order to function better. He says, "We will scream and cry, murder, run through the streets in agony, if it means some soul will be moved, moved to actual life understanding of what the world is, and what it ought to be." Amiri Baraka also wrote poetry, drama, fiction and essays in a way that shocked and awakened audiences to the political concerns of black Americans.

Baraka also describes prominent Black leaders as being "on the steps of the white house...kneeling between the sheriff's thighs negotiating coolly for his people." Baraka also presents issues of euro-centric mentality, by referring to Elizabeth Taylor as a prototypical model in a society that influences perceptions of beauty, emphasizing its influence on individuals of white and black ancestry. Baraka aims his message toward the Black community, with the purpose of coalescing African Americans into a unified movement, devoid of white influences.

Besides, Barak, there are several other famous Black American writers such as: Nikki Giovanni, Sonia Sanchez, Maya Angelou, Hoyt W. Fuller, and Rosa Guy who have contributed to providing African American literature its due place. Giovanni is the author of numerous children books and poetry collections, including *Chasing Utopia: A Hybrid*

(William Morrow, 2013), *Bicycles: Love Poems* (William Morrow, 2009) and Acolytes (HarperCollins, 2007). These poems and poetry collections reflect Giovanni's views on the African-American identity. Similarly, Sonia Sanchez is the author of more than a dozen books of poetry, including *Morning Haiku* (Beacon Press, 2010), *Shake Loose My Skin:*

New and Selected Poems (Beacon Press, 1999) and *Does your house have lions?* (Beacon Press, 1995), which was nominated for both the NAACP Image and National Book Critics Circle Award.

African American Literature

The African-American literary tradition implies the fact that African American culture is the culture of suppressed people. The history of African American people is marked with slavery (1619-1865) which is characterized by continuous dehumanization, humiliation, racial segregation, and exploitation. African-Americans were viewed as people with no history, no cultural heritage, no tradition, and no identity in white America. For centuries Europeans and Americans advanced racial theories of inferiority, which ascribed African Americans to the lower species and ignored their ownership of cultural, ethic, and linguistic values. African-American poetry includes many themes such as cultural guilt, marginalized identities and rootlessness.

Moreover, Black feminist thought while empowering African American adolescent girls to seek and define their own identities, simultaneously emphasizes collaboration and cooperation for the benefit of a collective voice and experience (Collins, 2000). Defining an identity also includes the acknowledgement of self-defined sexuality and expression, as well as the relentless struggle to eradicate violence (domestic, societal, and institutional) and sexual abuse and exploitation. "To be able to express the range of one's voice to express the totality of self..." while negotiating and reconciling "internally defined images of self as African American women without objectification as the Other" is primary (Collins, 2000, p. 99).

In fact, African American literature embodies novels, poems and plays showing the status of race as a whole. The writers' works reflect their identities (Warren 05). Explorations in the stream of novel writing have become established with importance on their finding and preparation of new talents. African American novel writing has taken shape down the ages, transforming their own and other literary cultures. African American literature presents a wide range of writings from the colonial period to the present. This Afro – American literature is related to different literary periods.

The term African- American studies refer to the literary tradition of the USA which has its roots in Africa as well as in America. During the colonial period, African Americans launched their literature in North America. It represents the divided self of Africans who were forced to go to colonial America. They were lost between their home land and their new identity. This custom emerged amongst chaos caused by colonization and slavery endured by the Africans in America. Some of them survived and the others died because of sickness and suicide. The inhuman condition in which these slaves lived and the exploitation of their right to live their own life is all well brought to focus through their literature. Andrew Jarret in 'A companion to African American Literature' says, 'One of the captured slaves who were transported to colonial America was Phillis Wheatley.' In her writings, she focuses on the contrast between slavery and freedom (Jarrett 22).The writers of this period sought to insist that the black Americans be given the same human rights as the white Americans. In 1773, *Poems on Various Subjects* is the first book by Wheatley shows that black Americans were not inferior to the Whites in art and culture.

Due to the issue of racism, many African-American writings were not recognized as authentic works such as Frederick Douglass and Harriet Jacobs. Through poetry, letters, sermons and slave narratives, African American literature of the colonial period was a means of breaking the bonds of slavery. In New England, those slaves who were close with their masters' families exchanged stories and experiences with the audience. They described their lives before slavery in Africa and their daily activities. They portrayed the suffering felt by husbands and wives separated from each other as well as the separations of brothers from sisters and children from parents. African-American slaves were prohibited from learning some skills such as reading and writing. Thus, they used their creative abilities such as songs, folk tale and oral storytelling to talk about slavery. These works incorporate the dialect of early black Americans (Smith & Jones 07). The issue of slavery and the revolutionary war led to the development of African American writings. Their poems and letters reflect the African - Americans' suffering.

In the wake of the anti-slavery movement in the nineteenth century, accounts of slavery by fugitives from the South dominated African American literature. During this period, many black slaves focused on the narration of their stories such as Frederick Douglas, Harriet Jacobs, and William Well Brown. Literature at that time was an instrument for the abolition of slavery. It consists of abolitionists' poems and slave narrations which show injustice and bondage of slavery. Fredrick Douglas *Narrative of the life of, Fredrick Douglas, an American Slave*, published in Boston in 1845 describes his life during slavery. This was later expanded into two more volumes representing the experiences of the entire slave class. The narrative differs from the earlier narratives by not being just autobiographical, but rather gives a severe critique of the American society. Douglas works through a pattern of resistance, endurance and survival.

The Antebellum period gave a chance for feminist writers to participate in the fight against slavery with black men writers. Two other noted narratives of the period are William Wells Brown's *Clotels* or the *President's Daughter* (1853) is the story of light-skinned African American woman, who dies trying to save her daughter from slavery. In 1861, the Civil War broke out between the North and the South over the issue of slavery. Therefore, African American writers speeches, narratives, poetry and novels served for breaking the Civil War (Brown & Webb 103). A few years later, Harriet Ann Jacob's *Incidents in the Life of a Slave Girl* (1861) an autobiography by an enslaved African American woman,openly describes the experiences of sexual exploitation of women during slavery. These narratives stood as the predecessors to the fiction that was to follow.

Frederick Douglass shows the importance of oral tradition in African American literature. He illustrates the relation between the abolitionist movement and literature in the nineteenth century. With the increase in the success of white fictions, the black writers were impelled to print in 1853. Harriet E. Wilson brought about an education by publishing *Our Nig: Sketches from the Life of a Free Black* (1859). It was considered the first novelby an African American. This autobiographical fiction describes the brutality undergone by the African American amidst segregation's trap. In the late 1850's Martin Robison Delany published his *Blake or the Huts of America* (1859-1862), whose hero plots a slave revolt in the South. This was the most politically radical novel, messianic in theme and characterization. The rhetoric follows the style of the early slave narratives. The variety of African American literature of the antebellum period concerned speeches, plays, novels and poems. These black writers invented a trend of their own. They used Black English for the speech of the black characters in their fiction. All these novels both in theme and style were preoccupied with the struggle of the black Americans for liberation from racism and classism.

The Era of Reconstruction

Despite the abolition of slavery, the United States was not able to realize the blacks' dream to be equal. Thus, African - American writers continued the discussion about the theme of slavery. In the Reconstruction era, there was a great emphasis on education and literacy for the purpose of obtaining freedom either socially, economically or politically. Black slaves were illiterate. For this reason, many schools were established to teach the writing and reading skills (Worth 05). The study of African American literature was given a serious consideration only after the Civil Rights Movement to mark this era of reconstruction. Consequently, there was an increase in freedmen's schools, black colleges, clubs and presses signified the use of education as a means to uplift the African American race.

African American writers used their pen to defend blacks political freedom. This era of reconstruction was the period which saw the development in variety of themes especially in fiction. Themes stretching from historical to twentieth century modernism were highly explored. Smith and Jones state that, "Pan Africanism in the Reconstruction period gave African Americans a sense of pride in black history and culture and provided a background to the emphasis on racial identity in literature of the Harlem Renaissance" (Worth 115).

The novel was considered an instrument of social analysis, confronting prejudices and stereotypes, focusing on changing the conditions of the Blacks. It was a period of active participation in literary movements like realism, naturalism, colour fiction and modernism. In fact, during this era of reconstruction, many writers attempted to integrate the oral and written traditions by incorporating black dialects in their literature. They used vernacular expressions in their works to capture the voices of the audience. Innovations like meta-narrative and transgressive blending of different genres came forth. Writers like Charles W. Chesnutt, Pauline E. Hopkins, Paul Laurence Dunbar and W.E.B. Du Bois (1868) explored varied themes like realism, folklore, family Sagas and Utopian longings for a better future. This reconstruction era brings out the great writers like Booker T. Washington (1856-1915), Anna Julia Cooper (1858-1964), W.E.B. Du Bois

(1868-1963), James Weldon Johnson (1871-1938) and Paul Lawrence Dunbar (1872-1906).

Booker T. Washington wrote a number of magazine articles and a history of black America in two volumes. His autobiography *The Story of My Life and Work* (1900) is the greatest work. The work carried out the personal experiences as a slave child and the problems he challenged to obtain the education. It could be considered a representative text of the problem of any African American of that time. Though born into enslavement, Anna Julia Cooper was the fourth Afro - American woman to receive a Ph.D. degree. Her first work *A Voice from the South by a Black Woman of the South* (1892), in which she brought outher belief that the Afro - American community could be improved by educating Black women. She showcased the power of Black female intellectuals. W.E.B. Du Bois was the first Afro – American woman to obtain a Ph.D. from Harvard University. He powerfully protests against racism. In literature, the struggle of the blacks for their rights began with Du Bois' *The Souls of Black folk* (1903). This book is a work of sociology rather than fiction, Du Bois describes the effects of racial prejudice on the culture of black Americans and provides an overview of African American life.

James Weldon Johnson devoted all his talents to the Black society. In 1900, he penned the song *Lift Ev'ry Voice and Sing*, for a school celebration. His song touched the total Black community of America, and earned the unauthorized title "Negro National Anthem". In bringing the essence of the sermons into poetry, Johnson assured the survival of the African oral tradition. Paul Lawrence Dunbar is famous for his black dialect, his poetry collections *Majors and Minors* (1895) and *Lyrics of Lowly Life* (1896), brought him worldwide fame. His novel *The Sport of the Gods* (1903) revealed the migration of Black people from the South to the North. He criticized the indifference of America to cultural violence by writing *The Fourth of July and Race Outrages* in the *New York Times*.

Some social factors such as the abolition of slavery, the gaining of suffrage rights for black men and the feminist movement led African American women to be a vital part of American work after the civil war. They asked for equality in their public and private lives. The novels produced from then onwards were based on segregation and social inequalities.

The era itself became an epitome of inhumane racist actions. Violence and lynching as the themes of the major works, disclosed the sufferings of African Americans. During reconstruction, African American slaves got freedom. As a result, they could receive education and owned land. However, by the end of the 19th century the reconstruction ended. The writers of this period not only recorded the life of the oppressed but also promoted intercultural understanding by undermining the stereotypical images of African Americans in the white minds.

The Period of Harlem Renaissance

The period of Harlem Renaissance is supposed to be the Golden Age of African American literature, "It is a movement in music, art, literature and politics from the early 1900's to 1940's, emphasized the importance of freedom- political, economic, social and artistic - for African Americans" (Smith & Jones 163). The Harlem writers were attracted by the atmosphere of New York since the main publishing houses were situated there. Hopkin's *Haga's Daughter: A story of Southern Caste Prejudice* (1901-1902) and Katherine DaviesChapman Tillman's *Beryl Weston's Ambition: The story of an Afro-American Girl's Life* (1893) was aimed at the Black audience. Harlem became the cultural center of the black people as New York City was one of the whites. The foundation of the Harlem Renaissance was based on the social and political thoughts of a group of young and talented individuals who were linked by a common black experience (Bloom 05).

During the period between 1900 and 1940, the demand for human rights increased. African American soldiers risked their lives in the First World War (1914-1918) for the sake of freedom, but they were not receiving the same treatment in the United States.

After their return, many African Americans called for the civil rights. The Harlem Renaissance, therefore, constitutes a large basis for the African American population. African American writers came from this city and the leaders of Harlem Renaissance were young artists and writers of the new generation. However, the African American novelists of this period realized the need for a dual audience as they saw the importance of inter cultural understandings. They wanted to prove their qualities and were proud of being blacks. Even tragicomic visions and heroic struggles were explored reflecting on the internal and external conflicts of the blacks at that time. With the rise in racial discrimination and oppression at the end of the century, the focus also turned towards the condition of the African American women.

Booker T. Washington's autobiography, *Up from Slavery* (1902) served as a guidebook to many of the writers of this period. In 1903 *The Soul of Black Folk* by Du Bois, asserted that through "work, culture and liberty" positive social change can be achieved. The writers of the era were Zora Neale Hurston, Dorothy West and Claude Mc Kay, who were the major exponents of the Black Women's Era. These writers represented the specific problems of Black women, whose experience of oppression was two folded because of being women and being black. They reflected the beauty of Southern vernacular (164). As an example, there is Hurston's *Mules and Men* (1925). It is considered as the best work that resulted from this era. The spiritual and religious notions of the women writers during this period turn their attention towards the standard of true womanhood. Development in the literary field was an outcome of variety in theme, culture and politics.

Projection of contemporary life, social realities and innovation in form and technology were the epitome of this new movement. Also, Harlem Renaissance led to the birth of black music, dance and literature including 'blues' and jazz. In addition, this was a phase of black culture's domination in America. According to Steven C. Tracy the term 'blue' denotes "to an emotion, a technique, a musical form and a song lyric and its influence can be manifested in a variety of ways from the very concrete to the very impressionistic" (122). The African American writers used the 'blues' – which reflected the individual experience and traditional values, as an affirmation of the black culture. Zora Neale Hurston's *Their Eyes Were Watching God* (1937) and John. A. Williams *Clifford's Blue'* (1965) are novels of this kind. This kind of music spread around the world not only in the United States. It gave a new spirit to literature especially to poems. One of the first books of poetry is *The Weary Blues*. This collection was written by Langston Hughes (1902-1967). It combined wordswith music (165).

During the Harlem Renaissance, The African Americans attempted to create a new identity for themselves. Literary activities flourished because of the growth of the Black literacy during the reconstruction. There were waves of gifted young writers coming to Harlem from across the land. The Harlemites' use of unique narrative strategies increased the publication of their texts. Their exploration of techniques like Bildungsroman and Kunstlerroman drew the African American novels from stereotypes generally concentrating on racial oppression. Claude McKay's *Bango a Story without a Plot* (1929) is considered to be the best among the works of this period. African American writers such as Angelina Weld Grimke and Marita Bonner improved drama and analyzed the theme of slavery (166).

The Harlem Renaissance is important because of its treatment of different issues ranging from feminism to black aesthetics. Thurman's *The Blacker The Berry: A Novel of Negro Life* (1929) considered race as the major integument of the capitalist system in America.The major theme of the novel revolves around the hopes of brighter future of primitive blacks of all nations. The African American fiction then onwards became the voice of educated Negro conflicting against the white injustice. It represents a milestone on the road from slavery to freedom for African American artists.

The Black community as the 'New Negro' strengthened the mission by starting a new school that flourished in the name of Harlem. Harlem was the pandemonium of all Black people who stayed together for basic needs. On the other side Harlem became literary center of African American writers for their writing activities. Not only for writing fiction, poetry, drama, and essay but also identified for rich cultural activities like sculpture, painting, music and dance.

Later it was considered as the Harlem Renaissance. A few decades were covered by Harlem Renaissance but in that small span it comprehended the important writers. The last part of the decade emerged an excess of writings by Afro – Americans, so that it obviously known as a movement of Renaissance. This Harlem Renaissance had produced a number of significant writers like Alian LeRoy Locke (1886- 1954), Marcus Garvey (1887 – 1948), Claude McKay (1889 – 1948), Zora Neale Hurston (1891 – 1954), Jean Toomer (1894 – 1967), Sterling Allen Brown (1901 – 1989), Langston Hughes (1902-1967), and Countee Cullen (1903-1946).

Alian Locke laid the foundation for the young writers at Harlem. He encouraged and supported the young Harlem writers. He helped Langston to publish his works. His incomplete work 'A study of Black American Culture' was completed by Margaret Just Butcher and published in the title *The Negro in American Culture*. Festus Claude McKay was the poet, who was born into the community of West Africa, got help from the English man and published his poems. Walter Jekyll inspired Mckay to write poetry. He wrote the poems about the life of Jamaican farm worker and the exploitation of the Blacks by White masters. "*The Dominant White*" and some of his poems were published in *The Liberator* and *Cambridge Magazine*. Zora Neale Hurston was the first woman to write and publish African-American folklore. In 1935 she wrote the collection of African-American Folklore

Mules and Men which was a famous and successful one in that period. Her best novel was completed after a trip to Caribbean "*Their Eyes Were Watching god*" is a symbol of victory of a Black woman over the powers of poverty and chauvinism. Jean Toomer was the only writer who spent all of his time with the Black rural community, on basis of this his major work *Cane*, which is an innovative work, brought him good reputation among the writers. He served as superintendent in charge in a school at Georgia. This helped him to move very close with rural black people. The innovative work *Cane* is a combination of prose and poetry sketches the theme of black urban and rural lifein America. Sterling Allen Brown was a black professor, folklorist, poet and literary critic.

He taught and wrote about African-American literature and folklore. Brown's poetry used the south for its setting and showed slave experiences of the African American people. Brown was known for introducing his students to concepts then popular in jazz, which along with blues, spirituals and other forms of black music formed an integral component of his poetry. Brown's poetic work was influenced in content, form and cadence by African-American music, including work songs, blues and jazz. Like that of Jean Toomer, Zora Neale Hurston, Langston Hughes and other black writers of the period, his work often dealt with race and class in the United States. He was deeply interested in a folk based culture, which he considered most authentic. Brown is considered a part of the Harlem Renaissance artistic tradition, although he spent the majority of his life in the Brookland. Some of his notable students include Toni Morrison, Stokely Carmichael, Thomas Sowell, and Amiri Baraka.

Langton Hughes is another leader of Harlem Renaissance. He helped many black writers to publish their works. He was interested in the blues and jazz of black music. As a child Langston listened attentively to these tales of slavery which were real stories. He was proud of this tradition and decided to make something to serve his race. Moreover, his poem, *The Negro Speak of Rivers* focuses on slavery and speaks about slaves who were sold down the rivers. In the fifties, his works expressed anger and a warning to the white claiming that if the black do not get their social justice, there might be an explosion of black violence. Count Cullen was a black poet who wrote for all mankind. He was not sure that the world may listen to a black poet. He was a romantic poet, his attitudes and his deep thinking influenced his personal life. He married Ida Mae

Roberson on September 27, 1940. After his death, his wife devoted her life to the activity of gathering materials about Cullen and other Negro writers (Perry 15). In his works, Cullen talks about love, beauty and life. Cullen's works make the readers feel the pain of being black in America. He wrote on universal themes quality and love. Throughout his lifetime, Cullen expressed the desire to be regarded only as a poet and not a Negro poet. In this sense, he told a New York reporter: "I want to be known as a poet and not as a Negro poet" (Perry 16).

Most of these African American authors of the Harlem Renaissance used realism. Many of them employed this literary device to fight racial issues. However, others used realism to portray African American life. American realism has been neglected by black writers as they gave more importance to the romantic works between the Civil War and First World War. The novelist Chesnutt claims that "there have been few realist fiction of African American life" (186). During this period, black authors did not focus on mainstream realism which exposes race relation in the South to maintain the white audience. The main realistic authors were Chesnutt, Pauline Hopkins and Paul Lawrence Dunbar. Thus, black writers produced a literature that portrays blacks as deserving equality with whites. As a result, they mixed between romance and realism (Jarrett 189).

The Protest Era (1940-1959)

The end of the Great Depression and the beginning of the Second World War represent the period of political protest for black Americans. The main purpose of the protest period is to eliminate racism. The writers were influenced by the research of socialists as Charles S.

Johnson, E. Franklin Frangier and Herace Cayton. The ideal of the novelists of this period was to reinforce rights of minority. The era of protest was either overt or covert. These protests were for the sake of gaining freedom from slavery (Smith & Jones 468). During this period, there was a great emphasis on the economic problems. The African American writers were very much aware of the slowly collapsing American economic system. Because of the depression, they experienced worse economic situation. African American writers had difficulties in obtaining funds to develop their writing career. So they became followers of the 'Chicago School' and the Communist Party. Novelists like Richard Wright, Chester Himes, Curtis Lucas, Ann Petry and William Gardner Smith were the forerunners of this literary movement. Richard Wright's *Native Son* (1940) and *The Long Dream* (1958) are identified as protest novels where these two novels portrait the life of middle class or working class are often provoked by hunger, fear and sex.

The reconstruction era and the Harlem Renaissance had not only strengthened the black man's credentials as great literary artists, but also had improved their aesthetic perception towards orienting themselves into various branches of realism called naturalism and modernism. Similarly, this exclusive period covering two decades from 1940 to 1960 could be hailed as a modernist era of African-American literature.

Black authors of the period were concerned with how to live with whites rather than going to Africa to escape from racism. As an example, Margaret Walter's poem, *For my People,* expresses pride in African American culture and revealed realities of racial oppression.This poem marks the new era for black women poets who had not published poetry since 1918 (Smith & Jones 470). The African American writers also experimented with new forms of writing. The novels published during the period 1950's – 1960's show the development in rediscovering myth, legend and rituals. Novels by Ralph Ellison and James Baldwin stand as the forerunners of this period. They followed the nineteenth century writers whose themes are fusion of history and myth and traditional and modern narrative forms. The African American novelist's intensity and creativity with which they have transformed their literary tradition is abundant. Today the rise of emphasis on the discovery of new talents in the area of African American studies has led to the wide recognition and popularity of African American writers. The great pioneers of the realistic school of thinking like Dorothy West (1907 - 1993), Richard Wright (1908 - 1960), Ralph Ellison (1914 - 1994), Gwendolyn Elizabeth Brooks (1917 - 2000), James Arthur Baldwin (1924 - 1987) and Lorraine Hansberry (1930 - 1965) served as the pre Black arts movement's writers who not only laid the foundation of a new strain in literature, but also paved the way for new experiments during the second decade of the Black Arts Movement.

Dorothy West wrote her first story at the age of fifteen. She started to sell her stories to *The Boston Post*. People praised her for the first novel *The Living is Easy*. She had written more than sixty stories and published in the *New York Daily News*. Richard Nathaniel Wright was the first writer of the twentieth century who provided black literature realistic techniques. Writers such as Richard Wrights put emphasis on the black experience, violence, hostility and colour. These themes became more prominent in this era. During the twentieth century, black literature needed realistic techniques. This is what Wright employed in his short stories. He uses naturalist techniques to describe the social and psychological pressures on his black hero like he does in his novel *Native Son* which introduces a black protagonist, Bigger Thomas, who is affected by the racial injustice of American institutions. This character influenced by his environment and treated with harsh manner. In this novel, many black writers describe blacks as victims of the white violence. However, Wright is the first one who claims that the social situation of the blacks leads them to become violent (High 215).

Gwendolyn Elizabeth Brooks was another poet who was a young child when her family moved to the South of Chicago. This city influenced Brook's works. In 1945, at the age of thirteen she published her first book of poetry, *A Street in Bronze Ville*, which presents the life of Americans in the Chicago suburb. In 1949, she published another collection of poems, Annie Allen, in which she tells the tragedy of the black life in America; she tries to present the Negroes. Another writer, James Arthur Baldwin, was born in August 1924 at Harlem, New York City, to an unmarried old woman called Emma Berdis Jones. Three years after his birth; his mother married David Baldwin who was a labourer Baptist minister. With him, she had eight children. Her husband became angry, abusive and violent. Thus, he terrorized his wife and children. This problematic relationship with his step- father pushed Baldwin to express his suffering. He died in Southern France in 1987 (Nelson 12). Baldwin's first novel *Go Tell It on the Mountain* (1953) is a short story about religion in Harlem.

In this period, religion created strong emotions and influenced People's life. On the other hand, it destroyed their ability to see the real life (High 217). Baldwin's second novel was *Giovanni's Room* (1956). Hence, these two novels deal with psychological problems.

In his novel, *In another Country* (1962), Baldwin expresses anger. This novel is his best work of fiction. This anger appears in other works such as the collection of essays entitled The *Fire Next Time* published in 1963 (High 218). Baldwin claims that non-violent methods can solve America's race problem. For instance, *Tell Me How Long the Train's Been Gone* (1968) is a novel in which he gives a warning to the white society.

Lorraine Vivian Hansberry was known as developed as a Black's representative to bring out the discrimination in America. In 1959, she published her first novel *A Raisin in the Sun* which brings out the racial discrimination in America. She wrote screen play forher first novel and sold it to Columbia Pictures. Her play won the New York Drama Critics Award made her the first black woman to receive it. This victory brought her name and fame among the Afro – American writers. Her second play *The Sign in Sidney Brustein's Window* was appraised by some intellectuals.

Literary Naturalism

Naturalism is a literary approach that explores the themes that have a relation with the growth of science in the late nineteenth century. "It meant that human behavior is solely under the control of heredity and social environment" (Hakutani 02). Naturalism had shown African American writers such as Wright, Ralph Ellison and James Baldwin. These writers tried to avoid rebellion, anger and protest. They were influenced by the philosophy of naturalism which helped them to develop their own versions of human rights. They attempted to liberate their fellow human beings from rules imposed on them. As an example, *Black Boy*, which is a novel written by Wright, has a great impact on African American literary criticism. Other black writers like Ellison began to believe that literary naturalism was a burden. It was not a technique for expressing African American reality.

The Contemporary Period: Modernism and Post Modernism (1960-Present)

The period lasting from 1960 to 1969 is referred to as the black aesthetics movement. This period was marked by the Civil Rights Movement, the Black Nationalist Movement and the Women's Movement. It was known as "Black Power Movement". During this period, black artists used multiple genres to make change in society. There was a rise in Black music and Black. Both Black Arts and Black Power concepts represent the African American's desire for self-determination and nationhood. For instance, Martin Luther King and Carmichael led hundreds of demonstrations through the Mississippi to explain the relation between blacks and American society. Politics and writing were inseparable. Activists focused on community control of schools, welfare rights, jobs and justice for the poor (Smith & Jones 659).

The African American women fighting for liberation from racism along with the black man had a dual task. They had to fight for the liberation of the black women from racism as well as both white and black male dominations. With the rise of this movement the voice of the black women writers gained more attention. Novelists like Margaret Walker, Mary Vroman Paule Marshall, Kirstin Hunter, Sarah Wright, Alice Walker and Toni Morrison helped to recognize the multiplicity of cultures embedded within black America. During the 1960's, black students asked for education relevant to their history of racial oppression. The proponents of the Black Studies Movement of the 1960's and 1970's claimed that the American educational institution had to be transformed (659). The activists cum writers of this period – Malcolm X (1925 – 1965), Martin Luther King, Jr. (1929 – 1968), Addison Gayle, Jr. (1932 – 1991), and Amiri Baraka (1934 - 2014).

From 1970 till the present, the American society changed. This new field in African American studies concentrated on discovering the diverseness of cultures within the Black American culture. Contemporary African American culture has attained an even higher standard today. The protest aspect of American literature has remained. In this period, black literature became an important part of university curriculum (Smith & Jones 743). In addition, African American women's voices began to be heard as a result of the women's movement and Civil Right Movement. Music was another means for African Americans to express themselves.

Modernism is a movement in art and thought that started in Europe and America in the late nineteenth and early twentieth century. Recently, it has been shaped by African American contributions primarily in the field of music with ragtime, blues, and jazz (Jacques Preface). Modernism emerged when a minority of African Americans lived among the whites in the cities by sharing less public space. It was the moment of the emergence of the racial ghettoes inhabited by African Americans. Artists used modernist poems and songs to transmit truth. One of the achievements of modernism is its ability to convey meaning in ordinary language. The tactility of language appeared through African American vernacular speech which is a part of the larger culture (Karl 17). Modernism represented the African American imaginary aiming at rethinking of the status of black culture within the American culture.

In the modernist era, the use of African American music in written works did not show the author's awareness of racial matters. In fact, music such as blues and jazz was used by authors for various purposes including social commentary and political protest. Thus, there is a connection between music and literature. Hence, music or jazz in particular reflected the hopes of African

Americans for finding a new life. Poetry, oral and slave narratives gave richness and diversity for the writing of the twentieth century. The Harlem Renaissance, Civil Rights and Black Arts Movements played a great role in the development of African American literature. Many well-known black writers appeared including Du Bois, Langston Hughes, Cullen, Wright, Ellison, Baldwin, Amiri Baraka and Brooks. They wrote about their personal experiences and the situation of the blacks in the American society. They used their fiction and poetry to end segregation and protect civil rights.

The neo-realism movement is related to European realism that was established in the nineteenth century. It describes life as it is actually lived rather than giving an idealized portrait of the world. It explains the material nature of life as it is. African American literature started to depict realistic life. Slave narratives and autobiographies were the main genre of this period. In this era, writings emphasized on the life of a society and the pressure of their community (Dickson-Carr 177). They were very important because they were based on truth and they were used to talk about the black in a racist country. Therefore, neo-realism in African American literature focuses on the real life experiences of black people (Smith 742). Contemporary African American neo-realism generally focused on the purpose of giving reflections of the life of African American communities. During this period, there was diversity in African American literature. All the genres were presented. Literature was a way for black Americans to defend their social situation. It has described the struggles of African Americans with slavery and racism. It contains the portrayals of African American experiences. This kind of literature has been given different names such as black literature, Negro literature, coloured literature as well as African American literature which was a response to the lived reality and the fact of segregation.

African American writers shed light on many phases of black life in the state of America. They were looking for their identities. Their works such as poetry, autobiographies, fiction and essays helped to form the African American literature. Consequently, black writers made a change by affecting their social reality and the literature that had been produced in response to it. The latter witnessed a change from the period of slavery to the present century. The writers of Harlem Renaissance were influenced by the style of European and American literature (High 212). They created works of high quality. The most famous African American women writers of the twentieth century are Maya Angelou (1928 - 2014), Toni Morrison (1931 -), Toni Cade Bambara (1939 – 1995), Alice Walker (1944 -), Ntozake Shange (1948 -) and Gloria Naylor (1950 – 2017).

Maya Angelou was born on April 4, 1928. She attended George Washington High School. She studied dance and drama at the California Labor School. Three weeks later after completing school, at the age of 16, Angelou gave birth to her son, Clyde. She writes about these events and the first 17 years of her life named, *I Know Why The Caged Bird Sings* published in 1970. Her autobiography brought her fame all around the world. The book won popularity and was nominated for the National Book Award. Her poetry book, *Just Give Me A Cool Drink of Water 'Fore I Diiie* (1971) received a Pulitzer Prize nomination.

In 1973, Angelou started to write for television. Moreover, she wrote articles, short stories, poetry and autobiographies. The hope for freedom represents one of the major themes that appear in Angelou's work. The Caged Bird symbolizes this theme as it depicts a voice of a protest. Angelou's writings show the realities of racism and the ways the African Americans have resisted oppression. She depicts hopes and compassion in her books. She also focuses on the theme of motherhood and the relationships among African American women.

Toni Morrison is a great writer who concentrates on black women issues. Her parents implanted a sense of heritage through telling traditional Afro – American folktales. She began writing fiction as part of an informal group of poets and writers at Howard University who met to discuss their work. She attended a meeting with a story about a black girl who longed to have blue eyes. Later, she developed the story as her first novel *The Bluest Eyes* (1970). In

1975 her novel *Sula* was nominated for the National Book Award. Her third novel *Song of Solomon* (1977) brought her national attention and won the National Book CriticsCircle Award. In 1987 Morrison's *Beloved*, inspired by the true story of runway slave Margaret Gamer, became a critical success. When the novel failed to win the Awards, critics and writers protested the omission in their writing that was published in *The New York Times* on January 24, 1988. In a short span, *Beloved* won the Pulitzer Prize for fiction and the American Book Award. The same year Morrison took a visiting professorship at Bard College.

In May 2006, *The New York Times Book Review* named *Beloved* the best American novel published in the previous 25 years. In 1993 Toni Morrison was awarded the Nobel Prize in Literature. Morrison was honoured with the National Book Foundation's Medal of Distinguished Contribution to American Letters, which is awarded to a writer who has enriched our literary legacy over a life of service. In 1996 the National Endowment for the Humanities selected Morrison for the Jefferson Lecture, the US federal government's highest honour for achievement in the humanities. Morrison played a vital role in bringing black literature into the mainstream by editing books of authors such as Toni Cade Bambara, Angela Davis and Gayl Jones.

Toni Cade Bambara was admired by Toni Morrison and many other authors because of Black English. *Gorilla, My Love* her first story collection written in Black English and published in 1972. As a social worker Toni Cade Bambara joined at Harlem Welfare Center and edited two anthologies *The Black Woman* and *Tales and Stories for Black Folks.*In 1980, she wrote her first novel *The Salt Eaters* which portrait the inequality and oppression of the African American Communities.

Alice Walker, who grew up with an oral tradition, listening to stories from her grandfather Alice Walker began to write privately, when she was eight years old. She was accidentally wounded in the right eye by a shot from a gun by one of her brother, the parents could not take their daughter to a hospital for immediate treatment. They reached the hospital after a week later, she had become permanently blind in that eye. She felt like an outcast and started to read and write poetry. When she was at the age of fourteen, the scar tissue was removed from eye. This incident taught her to be patient and notice the relationship of the people. After high school walker went to Spelman College in Atlanta and later transferred to Sarah Lawrence College. She started her carrier as a writer by writing articles for journals and her first book of poetry was written at Sarah Lawrence.

In early 1960, Walker met Martin Luther King Jr. when she was at Spelman College, she was inspired by King, who encouraged her to join the Civil Rights Movement. She took part in the 1963 March on Washington and volunteered to register black voters in Georgia and Mississippi. Alice resumed her writing career when she joined Ms. Magazine as an editor and published an article in the same magazine *In search of Zora Neale Hurston*. In 1970 Walker published her first novel *The Third Life of Grange Copeland* which sketches the life of Grange Copeland, an abusive, irresponsible sharecropper, father and husband. Her second novel *Meridian* was published in 1976, a semiautobiographical narrative based upon her experience in the year 1960 related to racial, social and sexual harassment that the Civil Rights era gave her.

In 1982, Walker published a novel, *The Color Purple* which narrates the life of a young troubled black woman fighting her way to dwell in the society, not only by the white racist culture but also by the black patriarchal culture. She coined the term 'Womanism' to mean Black feminism. As a leading figure in the liberal politics, she focused on the struggles of black women and their lives in a racist, sexist, and violent society in her writings.

Contemporary novelists usually focus on romantic and realistic fiction. In their works, they use dialect such as Harper's Century and The Atlantic. African American writers rely on folk traditions of masking to convey ideas for the black audience and provide the white audiences with surface meanings. Writers like Richard Wright, Langston Hughes, Ann Petry and Gwendolyn Brooks developed their craft. Thus, African American literature succeeded to capture the attention of the public. Literature includes traditional genres such as prose, poetry and drama as well as films and music. "The Black Arts movements gave rise to a set of journals like Negro Digest, the Journal of Back Poetry and Third World Press. This movement influenced cultural production in music, theater, art, dance and literature" (Andrews 471).

Contemporary African American writers began to redefine and change literature using models not only from European and American tradition, but also from their own distinctive oral forms. The poems, short stories and novels of the contemporary period represent creative writing. Each writer has influenced African American literature. These writers used folktales, "spirituals and blues within the traditional framework like Langston Hughes's poetic use of blues to redefine stanzas, or Amiri Baraka's recreation of the short story as a jazz composition" (Jones 01).

The twentieth century witnessed an explosion of African American writing and an expansion of the subjects of black literature. Since the 1970's, it has become difficult to generalize the major themes of the contemporary period. However, the most important subjects include the rise of African American writings, "the reclamation of history, the resurgence of autobiography, the rise of black gay literature and lesbian literature" (Andrews 471). The era of literature from the 1970's to 1990's begins and concludes with a black feminist note. After 1986, Sonia Sanchez, June Jordan, Lucille Clifton, Jayne Cortez and Nikki Giovanni produced books of poetry reflecting black women's position. Alice Walker's second book of poems entitled *Revolutionary Petunias* (1972) has preceded these fame-making novels such as *The Color Purple* (1982). As a result, the term "womanism" was coined to describe a feminism concerning women of color. This feminism was representative of the sexual, social and spiritual lives of black women (Booker 14). The era brought the publication of Ntozaka Shange's *Choreo poem* (1975), Michel Wallace's *Black Macho* and *The Myth of Superwomen* published in 1978 (Flora & Mackethan 18).

They discussed many topics that African American writers have often neglected such as domestic abuse. "Their works form a bridge between black arts and feminist literature that has had an impact on the African American literature of the Contemporary period" (Booker 14). These contemporary writers continued to write black literature that has a long and rich tradition; "the years of black anger are not over as there will be new explosions in the coming years" (High 221). During the eighteenth and nineteenth centuries, African American literature developed. The twentieth century marked the most productive period in African American literary genres since black authors have created remarkable fiction.

They won some literary prizes in the United States and in the world. In addition, this period saw the development of African American literature that became an institutionalized field within the area of historical and literary studies.

African American literature is widely known. By 1990, African American fiction became famous through Alice Walker's *The Color Purple* (1983), Toni Morrison's *Beloved* (1987) and Gloria Naylor's *The Women of Brewster Place* (1982). During this period, African American fiction had the chance to be read and appreciated. African American writers produced popular literary genres; they have reached wide audiences. Thus, African American literature embodies important foundational works. In fact, horrors of slavery, segregation, and discrimination fostered the continuity of black literary imagination in the late nineteenth and early twentieth centuries. Black writers reached a high artistic level especially in the 1920's as the Harlem Renaissance represents an outpouring of creative themes that were not produced before. In addition to this, "black writers of the late twentieth century turned their attention to history which constituted an important topic" (Miller 03).

Literature Review

Gloria Naylor, like many other African – American women writers, has been the focus of study among research scholars. Several books and articles have been written on this writer. In view of that fact - Self Identity, Protest, Motherhood, Sisterhood,

Black Feminism, Racism, Slavery, Portrayal of Afro – American Community, Women Quest, Violence, Ethnicity and Self Recuperation have been the themes of most of the researchers. These are the subjects which have been focused by many researchers but in this books, the researcher focused on the artistic skills of the writer.

In such a literary situation, the writer chosen for this research work, appeared as an influential Afro – American writer. Even though Naylor comes in the same category of other writers, and shares a few of their emotional responses, she deviates and shows the difference from other writers in different ways. It is true that Alice Walker and Toni Morrison were the great inspiration of Naylor however her uniqueness in writing exposes the distinction in her sensibility. *San Francisco Review of Books* attests Naylor as "Gloria Naylor's novels place her securely in a select circle of contemporary American literary luminaries, best circumscribed by writers like Toni Morrison, Alice Walker and Ntozake Shange."

Some critics have conceded the comparison of Naylor's works with the writings of other Afro – American female writers even with Alice Walker and Toni Morrison. Her novels usually contain portions of her own life and ancestral part in the common form of places, names and stories. Her characters and places are linked with each other in all her novels. Starting from her first novel, the characters and places in a novel becomes very important characters and places in the next novel. All her novels reflect an ethical and spiritual emotional responsibility to the society. She is great at creating the corrupt imaginary worlds in which her characters have to find some kind of a shelter to be secure.

The researcher is impressed by her work because she herself is a part in all her writings. She is respected in both academic circles and well recognized in the field of art and culture. She is correctly acknowledged for verbalizing the rights of women and other social problems. As to praise Gloria Naylor the *Detroit Free Press* states:

"Naylor's prose makes readers want to shout for joy about the power of love and the strength of language.... Naylor is a master at creating an emotionally charged page – turner."

A Critical Companion is full-length study by Charles E. Wilson, Jr. (Spring 2001) about Gloria Naylor. It appeared after the complete studies by Whitt, it is somewhat weaker in conditions of furthering the cause of critical approach into Naylor's work. This study begins with a brief life history of Naylor, her place in literary legacy of Afro-American writers followed by a detailed account of each novel. The advantage of this study is based on the assessment of *The Men of Brewster Place*. Wilson is the next critic who has given us keen insights on Naylor's fifth novel in his study. He acknowledges Naylor's way of transforming her worries in the characters with confines in her representation of Afro-American experience, he analyses *The Women of Brewster Place* with a feminist view and for *Linden Hills*, he picked intertextual analysis. For *Mama Day*, he chooses the psychoanalytical structure and for *Bailey's Cafe*, he uses the deconstruction approach. Naylor's stories have continually challenged all hard work at sinking her art and image to any canon, values or theory. Thus, approaching her artistic world with a permanent lens is like reducing the barrier of the authenticity as projected by Naylor in her own method.

Sunayana Mishra in *Feminism in the novels of Gloria Naylor* (2002) studies the feminism in all novels of Gloria Naylor. After meticulous study of this books, all the chapters explain that the novels of Naylor are about Black women and who have experienced tortures. These women characters are not just role models for black community but they are the characters who courageously face problems and survival in the male chauvinistic world. Naylor consider herself a feminist but she wants to be a different feminist to discover a new light with a new colour. This hope is evident in all her novel. Naylor states in her *In Search of Sanctuary*, "Feminism is for me the simple belief that all human beings, regardless of gender, are equal."

Payel Dutta Chowdhury in *Portrayal of the African American Community in the novels of Gloria Naylor* (2006) states in the conclusion chapter, any portrayal of the community demanded grappling with crevices at various levels and this is apparent in the works of Naylor and contemporary writers. The first novel of Naylor portrays the traditional values and communal bonding for the Afro – Americans as a resistance to oppression from different sources. The second novel portrays the soulless people struggling towards the better financial status for their future. In third novel Naylor has changed her view of the power of the community as a refuge from oppression to a community bonding as empowered by folk tradition by nature and by abiding spiritual forces.

V. Kundavi in her dissertation *Black Feminist Consciousness: The Healing Matrix in Gloria Naylor's Quartet Novels* (2007) examines the healing matrix in the novels of Gloria Naylor. Naylor takes up a new literary environment of conjuring for her unchaptered third novel Mama Day. In the fourth chapter of this books Naylor uses the art of conjuring to link the cultural past for supporting the mental and physical empowerment of her Afro – American Diaspora women. The conjurer, who is personification of all motherly qualities has established by Naylor as the spirit of Africa to the materialistic world and a feminist consciousness by affirming an identity to her writings. Naylor has mythical and matriarchal healing and Black identity in *Mama Day*.

Deepti Bagwari in her books *Element of Protest in the Novels of Gloria Naylor* (2008), studies protest as a weapon to assert one's identity and to attain dignity. A thorough reading of this books analyses that protest is an effective tool to generate change and also highlight the plight of the exploit. The author has registered her voice as "Protest is respected, celebrated, and analyzed as a source of inspiration because it is essential for survival.

In the conclusion chapter Deepti clearly explains that Naylor as a successful contemporary Afro – American women writer has multi-dimensional representations of male and female that brought her appreciation with the publication of *The women of Brewster Place* and *The Men of Brewster Place*.

Mohammad Hassan Gholampour in his books *Interrogating the Notion of the Self and Identity: Women in Novels of Gloria Naylor* *and Paule Marshall* (2012) analyses the journey of Black woman's empowerment. A close reading of Naylor's *Linden Hills* in Chapter III of this books shows how Naylor knowledgeably converses the causes of racism and gender relations on female Black identity. Naylor's demonstrative journey of Willa in *Linden Hills* took her to the past and to the life of other oppressed people like her. This journey gives Willa self-confidence and results in self – actualization. To construct such a creative communal identity, Naylor finds the independent African - American society within the governing White society to provide a chance for her women characters to get development in the absence of racist oppression. The major theme of Afro – American writers in their works is the theme of Black Identity and attainment of self-actualization.

Saroj Bala in her books *Development of self: A Study of Women Characters in the Novels of Gloria Naylor* (2016) analyzed the self-development of black women in the novels of Gloria Naylor. In this books, chapters II to Chapter V deal with the development of women by themselves. As the chapters named by the researcher show the focus of author about the black women in the society. Self and Individual - '*The women of Brewster Place*' deals with seven different women and their problems, and how they faced the difficulties because of being women, black and poor, Self and Family – '*Linden Hills*' the author allows the readers to take a journey through Linden Hills to look into the lives of the people to understand the crucial setting of the characters and their behaviour. Kinship and Community – '*Mama Day*' is set in a black island called willow spring where the characters keep moving in and out of the island, Self and Nature– '*Bailey's Café* is the interwoven stories full of pain and despair. Thus, Naylor has successfully represented black woman's life among the society and outside of the black community. The researcher clearly says that Naylor reveals the importance of respecting nature as living entity and works of Naylor are not meant only for the purpose of reading.

Prashant Connodgia in his books *A Study of African American Community in the Novels of Gloria Naylor* (2016), tried to prove that Gloria Naylor as a writer who has given a new name, a new definition to blackness and she tries to assert the authenticity of all female experiences as transcending the familiar constraints in her writing. In the sixth chapter the researcher sumps up that the black woman's quest for self-identity, self-awareness, self-empowered that has been materialize by Afro-American writer's desire to build and redefine the lives of black women. The researcher states that Naylor is a part of and yet apart from black aesthetics. She belongs to that part of black aesthetic that demands plurality. She does not give us one view point, one version, one truth, one perspective.

In a recent study **K. Valli** (2017) tracked the idea how African American identity came into use and resulted in the loss individual self-identity. The author describes slavery as a thing of the past but it has not been completely wiped out. It still exists in the minds of the people. The migrants know that that they must fix their roots in America even though they were Africans. They cannot return to their native land and now America is their homeland but they are neither Americans nor Africans and have a new identity - African Americans.

In another recent study, **Sonal and Singh** (2018), found the roots of multiculturalism Naylor's novel *The Women of Brewster Place* that contributed in creating a mixed, socio-cultural environment. Naylor through the depiction of the plight of women discusses multi-cultural issues affecting the social environment, particularly the black women. This study asserts the necessity of studying such multicultural issues in the African American context in order to resolve issues of personal identities, sexualities and psychological degeneration.

CHAPTER THREE

The Women of Brewster Place: The Search for a Home or Blending of Lives

"Time's passage through the memory is like molten glass that can be opaque or crystallize at any given moment at will: a thousand days are melted into one conversation, one glance, one hurt, and one hurt can be shattered and sprinkled over a thousand days."

-Gloria Naylor, *The Women of Brewster Place*

Introduction

The Women of Brewster Place is a novel of seven short stories strung mutually from one end to another end. Like pieces in a patchwork quilt, Naylor brings her characters one by one, each character adding to the color and completeness of the artistry in this novel. *The Women of Brewster Place* is a rational fiction and it depicts the predicament of the problems of the lifestyles prevailing in cities, which is deprived and colored. The residents are painstaking lower class, who are below the poverty line.

Naylor has created the artistic image of resilient colored women and their shared supportiveness in the novel. Naylor's women characters are not alone. Black women come to Brewster Place in search of peace. The reason for leaving is only lack of money. The residents of Brewster Place shared their struggle and take effort to live in unity with compassion and consideration. They stick on to Brewster Place as they found none to help out in the world.

Since these women happen to reside in Brewster Place, they have a narrow escape from the unfriendly and soul destroying forces of the city.

Artistic Characters of the Novel

The main characters and the title characters of each chapter are women and residents of Brewster Place. The seven women of Brewster Place are Mattie Michael, an unmarried mother who is relocated from her home and enforced to move to Brewster Place. Etta Mae Johnson,

a. playful, middle-aged woman who seeks for both pleasure and self-identity in various cities and with different men, but comes to Brewster Place when she has no money and men; Kiswana Browne, a middle class colored woman who discards her background and moves to Brewster Place and tries to help the inhabitants who live in Brewster Place under devastating and frightful conditions. Lucielia Louise Turner, who accepts ill-treatment from her husband. Cora Lee is another unmarried woman, who has attraction for babies, but ignores them when they get older; Lorraine and Theresa are lesbians, meet violence and refusal by the people of Brewster Place. All of the seven women struggle to live and form their lives under the conditions and surroundings that empower them.

The first and best narrative within the novel is Mattie Michael's. Mattie, along with several other characters, arrives in Brewster Place from her parents' home in the South. Mattie is the only daughter of a loving father, Mr. Michael. Her father works hard and accomplishes all her needs. One day Mattie reveals that she is pregnant and,

"...the torturing silence in the house was far worse than the storm that Mattie had prepared herself to take, her mother had told him about her pregnancy" (TWBP 19).

When Mattie becomes pregnant, her father kicks her out of the home. Understanding that she cannot marry the man who is the reason for her pregnancy, she leaves the family and plans to live with a friend in a nearby state and she delivers a male child. She views her motherliness as an entrance in the direction of self-actualization. From the beginning, Mattie is strong-minded to make a good existence for her child and herself, and goes out to find a job. She strolls thirty blocks on her lunch break every afternoon to see her child. "She had just enough time to rush in, pick him up, see if he was wet or marked in some way, and then go back to work" (TWBP 27-8). Mattie proves an excellent mother, loves her responsibility, though at times very hard. Mattie never reveals about the black ruffian, Butch, in front of her father because of terror and the dislike and hatred towards him.

The second story focuses on Etta Mae Johnson, now the situation is focused on the woman who gave protection to Mattie Michael over thirty years ago, when she was pregnant with Basil and now Etta Mae comes to Brewster Place to live with Mattie. Etta Mae Johnson, an old friend of Mattie's southern youth, a middle-aged woman look for both pleasures and a self-identity in various cities and with various men, but returns to Brewster Place when she has run out of money and men. Whereas Mattie has dedicated her whole life to her son and has never think of loving a man, Etta Mae has lived with an uncontrolled passion and at last has abandoned from her teenage years back in Tennessee. The character of Etta also reveals the communal approach and norms that regulate the lives of Southern blacks and whites. Etta apparently and knowingly rejects the sexual advances of a white male. Though her rejection results in the devastation of her father's belongings but the chief officer being a well-wisher suggests her to depart Tennessee for the sake of her existence. Unreasonably, to guard herself, she runs away. She realizes very soon that she would have to tackle discrimination and chauvinism in places other than Tennessee too. These threats compel Etta to shift from one city to another in search of a secure place to live without any commands and compulsions.

Naylor's picturization of the third women character Kiswana presents yet another example of friendship which Kiswana presents to Cora Lee in her own manner. She fights for the justice of Black women and in the zeal for honesty of Kiswana, Naylor points out that Brewster will not fall on any account. She is not in danger like others nor do not fight back, and has worn down by the continuous cycle of dislocation similar to others. Naylor's addition of Kiswana as an essential character in *The Women of Brewster Place* indicates the vast distance between women who have to live in women centered communities and those who choose to live with them in the Brewster Place. Kiswana's preference to live in Brewster Place is already a mark of freedom in the society. She is an exemption, while they are the rule and her privilege comes from the reality of a well-to-do community. Kiswana Brown wants to see her black contest gain equality in the white pursuit. She is portrayed as "naive, middle-class apostate given to revolutionary idealism" (Loyle Hairston 283). She joins a college protester group and to become aware with her roots, she changes her name from Melanie to 'Kiswana,' an African name. She moves from her hometown of Linden Hills, a society of black persons. She describes as

"white man's nigger ashamed of being black" (TWBP 85),

to the deprived, forceful, black neighborhood of Brewster Place. The encouragements of female affinity on Brewster Place make easy settlement between Kiswana and her wealthy mother.

The fourth women character, Lucielia Louise Turner, is also known as Ciel, the granddaughter of Eva Turner, who took in Mattie Michael when she was a young mother with no place to go. The story deals with the theme of the quarrel between the genders in the black community. She is Basil's early childhood playmate and Mattie is her second mother with whom she grew up. Though she has grown up with Basil but has not drifted away like him. She has married Eugene and has a baby girl. Eugene does not attach to a job or a place and leaves his wife for longer periods. In this story Naylor openly addresses the intention that black men need only to claim themselves as patriarchs in order to overcome deficit like it was in the case of Mattie that male authority was emphasized when her father beats her. The quarrel for marriage as the family ideal is disproved in the worried attempt by Mattie's adopted daughter Lucielia who too was a victim of her husband Eugene. To save this marriage, Lucielia attempts producing an unnecessary child, goes through a sacrificial abortion but had to face the trauma of the accidental death of their daughter Serena.

Cora Lee is the next woman character in this novel that has drawn huge attention of the critics. She is "an irresponsible black mother who loves children only when they are helpless infants and neglects them when they grow up" (Ranveer, 1995). She continues to have one baby after another and rejects them like old dolls when they are grown-up. The entire problem arises because of her ignorance of her role in the society Cora Lee is a wellbeing mother, who in her attraction for babies, her new mothering power is directed towards her children's education, and she has found a sisterhood in Kiswana which has raised her out of her loneliness. The contrast is Kiswana, who is worried about cultural identity and the mending of her African ancestry fails to identify her familiarity with her mother. Kiswana brings sisterly care to Cora Lee who is unstable in her mothering. Once Kiswana gets afar her own initial disdain, makes a payment to bring back Cora Lee's self-respect both as a person and as a mother.

The last two female characters in the book are Theresa and Lorraine. Being lesbians, both are professional women representing the female separation in the world of Brewster Place, Theresa and Lorraine create a render impotent threat to the men and a threatening expression to the women. At first, the two lesbians are accepted with some sort of hindrance, then are avoided and later, harassed. The women of Brewster Place refuse to talk to "the two" and even keep away from physical and eye contact. Theresa, already hard-edged toward "straight" people and their reactions to lesbians, appears unchanged by this behavior. But Lorraine, who cannot recognize the cause of other women for not accepting her and Theresa, strives hard to become a part of the group of women.

She does not fully admit her role as a lesbian because she wants the approval of the women. Theresa, in a vigorous of anger, discloses that Lorraine, not the inhabitants of all the other communities, has been the reason they are constantly on the move. Lorraine is harm when she is discarded and the two lovers fight between them. Although these women dwell in the same area, they too have various stories to tell about their life and the restricted choices that are offered to them as a result of their chase, gender and scarcity.

These characters in Naylor's *The Women of Brewster Place* are also those women who belong to a small Black community and this is their stronghold. Though these women come from various spheres of life, they care for each other and live a life of sisterhood in sisterhood. The characters are shown trapped in the society, discrimination and greediness. They fight against these traps and learn about humaneness, adjust and life. *The Women of Brewster Place* is identical with the pain and suffering of women who have been brokenand separated against on the race and sex. Women like Mattie, Cora Lee and Luciela are at Brewster Place because they have no other place to go and also have reached the end of the road. Their miserable lives have all reached this dead-end because of their racial and sexual identity. Brewster place is prevented from the rest of the city by a tall, brick wall. The avenue becomes the womb in which the people look after one another and search methods for endurance.

Plot: The Failure of the American Dream

The seven women characters are forced to come to Brewster Place as they found no other option in their lives. They come to Brewster Place after their personal tragedy. Soon they become neighbors, and then close friends and finally sisters. Brewster Place becomes a miniature American Dream or the world of the black community in common and their knowledge becomes the part of the experience of black community. They want to live with their own experiences, literary traditions, their memories and talents, and all these combine to make every one of them. A protagonist like Mattie Michael has her own voice. She is full of burning courage.

Etta Mae Johnson is of free nature and is a fashionable lady. Kiswana and Cora Lee are dreamers. Ciel learns rigid lessons in life and overcomes profound disappointment slowly due to Mattie's the protagonist's friendship. Theresa learns after losing Lorraine that living without each other's support and accepting will be rigid to accept. These women while see the American dream together, they also jointly share the bitterness and shattering of the same dream turning into a nightmare for each of them. The novel begins with Langston Hughes's poetic line:

"What happens to a dream deferred"? (TWBP 1)

The prologue is Langston Hughes' celebrated Harlem from his mixture of a "Dream Deferred". The poem reveals a direct warning of the dangerous impact waving through the group of people. American Dream continues to be held beyond the reach of the Afro Americans. According to Naylor this place is, "the bastard child of several clandestine meetings between the alderman of the sixth district and the managing director of Unico Realty Company" (TWBP 1). The American dreams of Brewster's residents make them to lead their lives in spite of their hardships. The dreams bond them and give a background of sharing and bond. Sigmund Freud's theory of dreams proposes that the various stimuli of our daily life force us to respond to them with dreams during our sleep at night (Freud Sigmund). But the daily routine of our life makes us to wake up in the morning. This theory is beautifully handled by Naylor in this novel, where she visualizes the fulfillment of the dream in every character, by redeeming themselves from the inequality they suffer in the American society.

The shattering of the dreams started with Etta engaged in illegal relationship with different people though at the same time she would discard sexual advances of certain whites as well as blacks. When she decided to move back to Brewster Place to meet Mattie, to rebuild her dream of reunion with her adopted daughter, Etta who was growing old, found American dream turning into a nightmare. In her younger days, she had considered that marriage could be the permanent solution, and she started to hunt for a suitable person. But soon she understood that there could be no everlasting relationship with men of her choice. But she got attracted to Reverend Morelands Woods, a black preacher, when Mattie took her to Church. She started dreaming to marry him and settle down to a respectable and wealthy years. She dreamt him to become her personal savior, who would deliver her from the sins of her past and guide her to a superior place. But after living with him, she understood that it was all just a dream and that he required only sex.

After that, she decided that she should not permit her courage to be broken. Reverend Moreland had destroyed her dream, but after facing that dishonesty, Etta understood her reality and started her life. Like Mattie, Etta is always outplayed by the person with whom she is concerned. When she returns to Brewster Place, she has lost her happiness, bravery and self-confidence but still there is someone waiting for her, it is none other than Mattie her best friend, who is always constant and the ease for Etta Mae. It seems Etta's dreams have been delayed but not yet destroyed. The American dream is alive but only for individuals.

However, in the American dream perspective, Etta Mae Johnson's story emphasizes chauvinist domination that women sometimes suffer even at the hands of their lovers. Her early life is filled with repeated rapes by a white man of her small rustic society. Etta Mae Johnson, places her last hope for a decent life on inviting Reverend Moreland T. Woods into wedding. She "... was a woman who was not only unwilling to play by the rules, but whose spirit challenged the very right of the rules to exist" (TWBP 59). Etta is sent out of the small town from which both Mattie and she come, stirring from man to man for good economic and prosperous living. She cracks the rules by accepting them with revenge. Like her male equivalents, Etta wants to ascend in the community level and she does it by using the equivalents as a product. Abandoned by Reverend Woods, Etta understands that she is cornered in Brewster Place and she has no place to go. Etta now again dreams of a guy who can shift her from the Brewster Place for betterment, but she is totally frustrated by the dream each time when the man irritates her. Every time She...

"laughed softly to herself as she climbed the steps towards the light and the love and the comfort that awaited ....But just as the pigeon she watches, fails to ascend gracefully and instead lands on a fire escape" in awkward, frantic movements (TWBP 74 - 75).

On another occasion in the novel, when Mrs. Browne visited her daughter, Kiswana's apartment on Brewster Place, it culminates with the two women realizing that their relationship marks another American dream being created. Mrs. Browne tells her daughter,

"You don't have to sell out, as you say, and work for some corporation, but you could [dream to] become an assembly woman or a civil liberties lawyer or open a freedom school in this very neighborhood. That way you could really help the community" (TWBP 84).

Despite her particular individual problems, Kiswana Browne is depicted as "a dreamy woman-child of black middle class," and a doubtful young African-American innovative, functions as a religious leader in this novel. She tries to get them interested in taking delight in themselves, their inheritance and their society. But Kiswana's dreams of a revolution will be put down by the discouraging actuality of Brewster Place and the awkward, worried actions of the people who are hectic and are merely trying to endure. However, Kiswana has a sense of dreaming about the functions of power because she has come from a place named Linden Hills which is focused on money and power. Started by her dreams, Melanie Browne of Linden Hills, thus changes her name to Kiswana and goes down to dwell with "the inhabitants" in Brewster place, dream of living a life like that of "the whites" who too had gone in the sixties to live in colored communities.

The story of Lucielia and Eugene create yet another story of a shattered American dream during one of the revisits of Eugene, Lucielia once again becomes pregnant but he compels her to abort the infant. Eugene becomes upset and exasperatedly shouts:

"What the hell we gonna feed it when it gets here, huh-air?

With two kids and you on my back, I ain't never gonna have nothin.

'Nothin', do you hear me, nothin!" (TWBP 95).

This outburst of the Dream shattered clearly shows Eugene's dissatisfaction due to monetary predicaments, though he is not careless but looking to overload himself without economy, and he shouts at Ciel and again chooses to move away. But Ciel begs Eugene to stay as her partner and as her daughter's father, helplessly trying to stop her dream to vanish away. She strives hard to stop Eugene to move away but all her actions go in vain. He yells upon Ciel that,

"I lost my job today, he shot at her, as if she been the cause" (TWBP 94).

The joblessness of the American Blacks was another issue that Naylor has inadvertently related here and it gets linked with the failure of the American Dream for the common man. Eugene's opposition towards his wife is openly linked to his constant joblessness. Unable to face the communal and economical realities that are dependable for his problems and unable to give the support for Ciel and his daughter Serena, he grasps Ciel dependable for his troubles.

The failure of the American dream that underlies the plot of this novel also indicates the suffering that black men and women felt by discrimination and economic devastation. Finally, Eugene compels Ciel's submission to his authority. At one instance, Ceil left the suitcase go before he jerked it away.

"She looked at Eugene, and the poison of reality began to spread through her body like gangrene. It drew his scent out of her nostrils and scraped the veil from her eyes and he stood before her just as he really was – a tall, skinny black man with arrogance and selfishness twisting his mouth into a strange shape" (TWBP 100)

Lucielia Louise Turner who had dreamt of love, from her boyfriend, daughter and unborn child, but her dream shattered with unwanted abortion, death of her daughter, and the rejection by her boyfriend cruelly marking the failure of the American Dream.

The dreamy saga of Cora Lee, another character in the novel, opens with a quotation from Shakespeare's *A Midsummer Night's Dream* (1595) "True, I talk of dreams/ which are the children of an idle brain/ begot of nothing but vain fantasy" (107). Cora Lee is important in discovering the uncertainty of the American dream and in setting up a division between dream as hopeless fantasy and as a supporting or transforming power. Cora preferred no other toys than a new baby doll every year. Her desire for dolls is indicative of the fact that she never grows up. She becomes a woman who repeats her dream and finds herself with a large, challenging family. Incapable to cope with the older children, she however continues to persuade her desire for the sweet and soft newborn. It is not until Kiswana Browne knocks on her door one day, seeking her help in getting a tenant's association where Cora Lee's life begins to transform. Kiswana invites Cora Lee and her children to an all black production of *A Midsummer Night's Dream* in the park at first Cora Lee is affronted, thinking Kiswana is important in her parenting, and then she uses her annoyance as inspiration. She brushes the children and restores their clothes in preparation for the big occasion.

In the park, Cora Lee is affected by the play, and an impressive. Kiswana's wish to change her neighborhood takes its initial root in the existence of Cora Lee and her children. Thus the American Dream seems to settle down in her life once again. She starts dreaming of fine jobs for her children "in insurance companies and the post offices ..." (TWBP 126) homes in Linden Hills - a middle class ambition. When her son asks her whether Shakespeare is black, she replies, "Not yet" (TWBP 127), remembering the awkwardly situation for having been beaten up for writing rhymes on the restroom walls. Cora Lee doesn't understand, that here urban authority is answerable for such living circumstances where her children have no liberty for themselves in a small residence. The play reflects the dream of Cora lee that she decides to walk her kids to school every day and to send them all to schools. She dreams of good education and jobs for her children. She believed that these may secure her children.

Naylor suggests here is that Cora is stimulated to imagine and dream. Kiswana has succeeded in issuing a space sisterhood to Cora Lee, a person with a search with the displeased and unattainable American dreams of Afro American women. Their sisterhood relationship is one more example of the capability of women to be in Brewster Place for each other, when men are nothing more than darkness. Cora Lee's new found sisterhood with Kiswana allows her to see the opportunity of an improved and brighter future. Naylor does not inspect the communal forces, which are accountable for the fruitless nature of many black women's lives in as methodical, and enlightening an artistic style in her novels. The Women of Brewster Place offers the author's discoveries of her characters' own responsibility in the tragedies of their life.

The last two characters, Lorraine and Theresa failed to weave any dream due to their lesbianism, which rejected them to be respected members even of their own black community. For the two, even the circle of sisterhood seemed to have shut. They are being shown not worthy of a dream of a good life, like other women characters of the novel. Lorraine was the first to understand the naughtiness of the people because as a pleasant woman, she begins to notice that her good wishes go unreciprocated. Hence, the above account suggests that though many of the women share comparable troubles and problems like the dealings with men and with other members of their society, each woman faces a distinctive situation that terms for a reply associated not only to the situation, but also to the character of the woman and knowing of herself and the transformation of the society.

Themes: Fractured Relationships

The seven women residents of Brewster Place are strained together in relationships with people around as they live on a dead end street and they share the general destiny. What Naylor suggests in the fractured relationship that each of these seven characters would try to weave around themselves?

The story of fractured relationship begins with Mattie's father who had warned her daughter about Butch and warned,

"...a no'-count ditch hound, and no decent woman would be seen talkin' to him" (TWBP 9).

Mattie commits fault and conceives a baby, the beginning of an illegitimate relationship. Mr. Michael beats her very brutally demanding the name of the man who has sneaked into his home and distorted the belief and faith, in the form of this child. They have hardly spoken but she is convinced that the baby does not really belong to her father. She does not expect her father to identify with the real reason of her pregnancy, and totally ignores and refuses to tell the secret. The father understands her silence as she has preferred to take Butch against him and in his anger, he tries to beat out what has harmed him the most.

The father is distressed to see her daughter's disobedience. His relationship with his wife Mrs. Michael too is very harsh since she has a soft corner for her only daughter Mattie. This signifies the aspect of the difference of outlook in every individual at the problem of child bearing and beginning of relationships. The negative approach of her father makes Mattie worn out. She works hard to promote her son Basil, and gives the best to him expecting nothing in return. Basil goes to college and easily falls into bad friendship and fails to think about his mother Mattie's hardships to nurture him. One day, Basil commits a murder and goes to jail. To get him out of jail, Mattie sells her house, which belonged to Miss Eva Turner, who was very supportive to Mattie in her hardship and tragedy, and after her death the rights of the house comes to Mattie. After this dreadful incident, Basil runs away leaving Mattie alone. Being detached and depressed, she thinks,

".....there just wasn't enough life left for her to do it all again" (TWBP 7).

Mattie's love for Basil is so strong that she crosses the line between vigorous love and harmful love. She does not want to protect her son at the same time she feels upset on seeing him taking wrong decision in life. She gives him everything and never wants anything except his love. When Basil is thirty, Mattie spoils him continuously so he has no sense of responsibility to his mother or society. She spends all her power and religious and emotional self into Basil. When Basil is blamed of killing a man after a clash at a bar over a woman, Mattie foolishly uses her residence to bring Basil from the prison. His choice is to leave the town. This forces his mother to move to Brewster Place. Violence and abuse are at the hands of men both white and colored (black). Loving fathers beat their lovable daughters ridiculous and send them out of the house. Mattie and her son are protected by Miss Eva, who receives her in as a daughter. 73

Despite her age Miss Eva remains the forceful amusing woman of her youth. She claims Mattie that she had "five husbands and outlived 'em all" (TWBP 32) and her old residence still burns with the laughter of her missing son's girl child, and the sparkle of cheerfully polished surfaces. She turns as mother to Mattie, Basil, and her own granddaughter. She connects all together into a family from the ruined city location. The immigrant discovers a secure space in Miss Eva and her home as she performs as the "predecessor". Miss Eva grasps the tenderness of life even after the prettiness and enthusiasm of youth have passed. Mattie recognizes, Miss Eva as the substitute of the mother. After Thirty years Mattie gets ready to take Miss Eva's place, she considers the messages the substitute mother taught her, and also in turn takes over the duty of protecting the weak women. However, Mattie has no house or family of her own.

When the two women travel from the South to North, the closeness and attachment between them helps to oppose the sexist, racist white humanity. Mattie's closeness with Etta acts as the best example of the way in which the South ensures the development and endurance of the immigrant in the city. Thus, Mattie in her whole life struggles without any emotional support and does her duties without any anticipation. Naylor has exposed different faces of male characters such as a heartless father, an abandoned lover and a useless son in Mattie's chapter. At the same time Etta extends some illegal relationship with different men in different places and environment. Even though she discards sexual advances of certain whites as well as blacks yet while running from one place to another, she happily makes some physical contact with different men. At last she decides to move back to Brewster Place to meet Mattie. Etta is growing old and so, she needs to settle down.

These lines portray the husband-wife relationship which has been afar the agreement and indicates the suffering from worry between black men and women caused by discrimination and economic devastation and overreacts that, "I'm fucking sick of never getting ahead. Babies and bills, that's all you are good for..." (TWBP 94). Finally, Ciel realizes that Eugene is totally selfish and self-centered. So she decides to deliver the baby and gives up the plan of abortion. During their argument, the baby Serena goes near an electric socket and gets electrocuted. After losing her child:

Ciel's whole universe existed in the seven feet of space between herself and her child's narrow coffin. There was not even room for this comforting God, whose melodious virtues floated around her sphere, attempting to get in (TWBP 101).

Though she attends to her infant children she has not the least viewing children when they are no longer babies. Her unawareness of the fact that they are weak in studies results mainly from her failure to provide sufficient control or motivation. There is no one to guide her till Kiswana arrives at the place. Cora's men are unimportant and survive as mere darkness. This is the township chauvinist power that acts upon Cora in the form of these men who burden her with infants. Even these men hurt her physically by fracturing her jaw. Once a man promised to marry her, but he never returned from a outing to the store to buy milk. "So Cora lives on welfare and accommodates the shadows in her bed for the brief sensuous pleasure" (Matus 132). Thus Cora becomes one of Kiswana's confront.

She thinks that marriage could be the permanent solution, and she starts to hunt for a suitable person. But soon she realizes that there can be no everlasting relationship with men of her choice because she is attracted to Reverend Morelands Woods, a black preacher, when Mattie takes her to Church, and dreams to marry him and settle down to a decent and wealthy years. She wants to become her personal redeemer, who will deliver her from the sins of her past and guide her to a superior place. But after living with him, she understands that it was all just a dream and that he required only sex.

Mrs. Browne relates to Kiswana a personal evidence of a mother's love. Kiswana trusts that she can have some outcome in this kind of society. They have no money, only the relationship that exists between the two as humans and as blacks. "Kiswana no doubt believes herself the epitome of radicalism until she listens to her mother's theatrical recounting of her proud heritage and commitment to the black cause. Suddenly, she comes to understand and appreciate the source of her own dynamism, idealism, and dedication to her mother" noted by Ebele Eko (145).

At the meantime, in Brewster Place the first meeting of 'The Brewster Place Block Association' takes place in Kiswana's residence, where Mattie, Etta and Cora Lee characters make an appearance for the first time in the novel. During the meeting when Lorraine enters the room, it crumbles as Miss Sophie's discourse doubts against her thought of Lorraine's relationship. But it is Mattie, who first feels uncomfortable with the subject matter of women who love each other. When she asks her friend Etta, what makes Etta and her lover unusual, Etta answers that they love each other the way a man and a woman love each other. Although feelings and awareness of Mattie's character prepares her as an example in the fatality of Lorraine , Naylor points at the fears of opposite gender for the women who are lesbians, even as she highlights the violent behavior, men do enforce upon them. Actually, Etta argues with Sophie about Lorraine and verbally abuse her condition that she would not be able to take notes but Sophie becomes irritated and answers,

"Listen here!'...' Why should a decent woman get insulted and y'll take sides with the likes of them?' Her finger shot out like a pistol, which she swung between Etta and Lorraine" (TWBP 144).

The above comment of Sophie makes Etta quiet and her silence carefully indicates her fear of being detested for she has previously made several illegal relationships with various men and which has been tolerated and unnoticed by the society. But the indication that she is lesbian would not be tolerated by the society anymore. Her silence also indicates her displeasure of homosexuality and lesbian relationships. Therefore, Lorraine, who is physically and emotionally separated by this incident, at last leaves the apartment and, "...fights an impulse to throw up."(Ranveer, op.cit, 123)When all other women criticizes Lorraine and Theresa for their lesbian love, Mattie says to herself love can "it's not so different, Maybe that's why some women get so riled up about it . . ." (TWBP 141).

Lorraine and Theresa thus represent the decisive obligation of woman to woman while their neighbors react to their relationship with the same communal rejection that drove them to this street in the first place. Like other human beings, they in Brewster Place put the same wall between themselves and Lorraine and Theresa. When the two appears the circle of sisterhood shuts for the moment. Etta Mae does not recognize the love between two women can be the same as the love between a man and a woman until Mattie says,

"I've loved some women deeper than I ever loved any man . . . .
And there [have] been some women who loved me more and
did more for me than any man ever did." (TWBP 141).

They accept this new alertness that women can love each other women more intensely than men. The weak and calm, glow skinned woman Lorraine looks for nothing more than to become closely associated with the rest of the women at Brewster Place. But she feels rejected by the women of Brewster Place as well as by Sophie's friends in the society. The only person with whom she can relate to and talk to is Ben, who tells Lorraine that she reminds him about his daughter. He is troubled by his memories, when his daughter was being raped and crushed by her White boss.

Although Lorraine lives with Theresa however she feels guilty and ashamed of their relationship. So, Lorraine defers by shifting the place. When Lorraine starts to face her, Theresa is annoyed and envious because she notices her lover's growing revolt as an effect of her friendship with Ben, an old drunkard and a caretaker of Brewster Place Though Ben becomes an alcoholic, a man of no large authority even on Brewster Place, He thinks that men as well as women can protect and care. Ben is one Brewster place resident, he says to Lorraine, "I got nothing, but you welcome to all that. Now how many folks is that generous?" (TWBP 149). Together Ben and Lorraine form a father daughter relationship until cruelty tears them separately. Ben is the father who has been betrayed and has lost his daughter, Lorraine is the daughter who has been thrown out by a denying father. Discarded of being a lesbian, she hopes that one day her father may accept her.

'The two' women's relationship escorts Sophie, a self-appointed correspondent of the activities of Lorraine and Theresa, to honestly deal with Lorraine. Sophie is one of the residents among them, who note the departure between 'The Two'. On a Late night, when Lorraine is returning home through the dark lane next to Brewster Place she is harassed and raped by a group of teenagers. Naylor's portrayal of this scene brings out the horrifying effect on the readers. The young man's elimination of lesbians varies from that of the other inhabitants of Brewster Place. Men to show their supremacy and power, these young men depend on their sex to prove their dominance. People who reject, plainly or silently their manhood is a danger to black women. Lorraine's thought is as the same at so she had stepped in. The community of the males also feels threatened by the lesbians. So to "validate in a world that was only six feet wide" (TWBP 170)

Symbolism: Communal Harmony

Naylor highlights Lorraine's rape as symbolic of supremacy, rather than sex. The group rapists, led by C. C. Baker, consign rape as a reprimand of lesbianism, a symbolic penalizing act planned to restore gender positions, both their own male supremacy and

Lorraine's role as a woman. They want her to discern them, not the female community. "Lorraine, rejected by the others is gang raped in a blood sacrifice brutally proving the sisterhood of all women" (Gottlieb 25). The rape is a physical as well as emotional horror. Loraine cannot get the recognition from young men to see her as a being, Lorraine's self-image move away from her senses:

Then she opened her eyes and they screamed and screamed into the face above hers—the face that was pushing this tearing pain inside her body. The screams tried to break through her pain inside her body. The screams tried to break through her corneas out into the air, but the tough rubbery flesh sent them vibrating back into her brain, first shaking lifeless the cells that nurtured her memory. Then the cells went that contained her powers of taste and smell. The last that were screamed to death were those that supplied her with the ability to love - or hate. (TWBP 170-71)

C. C. Baker needs to reclaim his power over Lorraine, and thus restore his status amongst his peers. Thus Naylor moves beyond this exclusively for personal motivation to display how the high communal restrictions upon young black men which leads to the expelling of their annoyance upon members of their own society, especially on black women. Naylor argues that these young men who have no other way of proving themselves as authoritative and with society, other than abusing a woman. C. C. Baker has re-established his logic of superiority as a male has forced the lesbian to have sex with him and his friends, devastating her rational and bodily integrity.

Kubitschek argues that Naylor shows Lorraine's destruction as the result of "concretely oppressive social conditions" (Subjugated Knowledge 47). The reader's empathy is entirely with Lorraine as a human being who has to endure a dreadful physical and emotional pain and strain. Lorraine and Theresa are analyzed as a threat by the Brewster Place people because of their sexual and cultural norms which have created a threat to the humanity created. This would replicate their perception of authenticity and their understanding of good and evil, and their behavior on right and wrong. All other residents are forced in their viewpoint that restricts their capability to allow weirdness.

Despite their differences, women in Brewster Place openly exhibit sexism and racism. Incident of Lorraine have entered the insensible thoughts of all Brewster's females, causing the dreams of both mothers and daughters to be troubled by the image ". . . the tall yellow woman in the bloody green and black dress" (TWBP 175). The characters of the individual sections of The Women of Brewster Place form, in response to Cora Lee's statement that a week of rain has failed to wash Lorraine's blood from the wall, a strong-minded and harmonious group working desperately to shred down the formation. These women,

. . . flung themselves against the wall, chipping away at it with knives, Plastic forks, spiked shoe heels, and even bare hands; the water pouring under Their chins; and plastering their blouses and dresses against their breasts and into the cracks of their hips. The bricks piled up behind them were snatched and relayed out of Brewster Place past overturned tables, scattered coins, and crushed wads of dollar bills. They came back with chairs and barbeque grills and smashed them into the wall. (TWBP 186)

In the portrayal of Lorraine, the most worrying example of the community's fanaticism of 'The two' is the rape of Lorraine by C.C. Baker's group. The gang's denial of lesbians differs from that of the other inmates of Brewster Place. The argument between Baker's gang and Lorraine becomes so miserable that this troublesome gang decides to conquer and want to defeat over women. In this course, they wield control and their dominance over Lorraine by raping her, "As they tear up this woman, her previous words that black people are all in the same boat reverberate with horrible irony." (Subjugated Knowledge). 'Please' is only repeating the word by Lorraine during the rape. Her appeal was for sympathy, understanding and most possibly for humanity but all pains go in vain, because there was no one to hear her voice.

After rape, Lorraine has thoroughly withered and destroyed. In the novel, one can see, Lorraine, as a black lesbian who cannot insist about her needs or needs for her sex and color which places her in a complicated position. Barbara Christian states,

In contrast to Walker and Shange, Lorde and Naylor consciously use the word 'lesbian' in characterizing their protagonists. Neither Lorde nor the lesbians of Brewster Place have been deeply hurt by men before they choose women as lovers. Rather, their choices go back to their adolescence and it s society, both men and women that hurt them because they have chosen to love women.

The chapter of Lorraine plays vital part in the novel. The innocent and harmless girl in an emotion and hopelessness kills an old man Ben, the one who was trying to help her during the rape. Ben as caretaker of Brewster Place believes his foremost priority is to help and take care of each resident of Brewster Place and so he strives hard to help her, but Lorraine unknowingly kills Ben viewing him as a one of her rapists. Thus, the story ends with the fatality of Lorraine and Ben. Among the seven characters of the Naylor's, Lorraine was the most crucial personality, who was raped by a group and after the dreadful rape she dies. As far as Lorraine is concerned, Naylor states:

Lorraine wasn't raped because she is a lesbian, they raped her because she was a woman...I feel very strongly that we as black people have to be there as nurturing agents for each other, male and female, female and female. And when that broke down in "The Two", I wanted to show how that could destroy the community. (Goldstein, 1983)

Naylor applies the balance in her story to increase the bond of kindness between Ben and Lorraine. Ben's daughter is lame and Lorraine is inner limp, which labels her as a victim, and the mannerism in her that reminds him of his daughter. Lorraine faces and tolerates male chauvinism, male ruin and most possibly male anger. After facing above predicament and hatred, she ends her life but her soul exists in the life of every inhabitant of Brewster Place, "Naylor uses the symmetry in the stories of Ben and Lorraine predictably, to develop the bond of sympathy between them. The banished daughter and the bereft and guilty father connect." (Matus

55)

The Women of Brewster Place is divided into three parts Dawn, seven women characters, and Dusk their struggles to endure and their realization after the battle. Dawn and Dusk in the novel are symbolic of Brewster Place's Dawn and Dusk. Of the seven stories, six are based on individual characters, while the final story is about the entire community.

Another symbol is wall. All these women dream of being united in order to eradicate the wall of Brewster Place, which is a mark of "dead-end street." (Ranveer, op.cit., 112) The women think that this wall separates them from the white humanity and civilization, and hence they wish to knock down the breach between white and black. All these women create their solid presence and show their trouble against permanent and predictable myth of a chauvinist and racist society. Symbolically, Naylor uses her introduction to notify, how and why the prospective of Brewster dried up like the regular "raisin in the sun" (Langston Hughes). The loss of Brewster Place's prospective comes in the figure of the wall. The construction of the wall is the work of some unnoticed power which has no contact or direct relationship with the real residents of the avenue. Naylor sums up in a single phrase accurately that,

"there was no one to fight for Brewster Place"(TWBP 2).

After demolishing the wall, the women of Brewster Place organize the party called 'The Block Party.' Though Brewster Place is rested around the seven women but everywhere they have to forfeit an intense charge for performance of the image of assortment in front of residents for equality, the women trudge out the wall of threat, the women show their power and courage against male chauvinism. It is Gloria Naylor, who uses Mattie, as a first and leading woman who expects to change the situation and conditions in the male dominated society. Brewster Place has radically changed after non-stop de-humanization and fight. The women are now identified with their own identity and the dreams now take its new form with more power, energy and objection in 'The Block Party'. By destroying the symbolic wall, Naylor determines that when women confirm unity, they can break the label of male and dominated fable of a chauvinistic society, wherein the wall becomes a strong symbol in the novel.

The novel ends when the Black women at Brewster Place revolt against their environment and with the help of their neighbors, tear down the walls of the dead-end street on which they are trapped". (Talks with America's Writing Women). 'The Block Party' is a significant chapter of the novel because of its exploration into the meaning of Black community. The novel ends with the death of Lorraine and Ben, a janitor of Brewster Place. Immediately after their death, the torrential rain has started and it continues throughout the week. In the novel, the rain represents the cry of black women which depicts their anger. When the rain stops, the black women understand the truth and reality of collective awareness which will ultimately lead them to passion and cheerfulness. The residents of Brewster Place are Black women, who are consistently deprived. Brewster Place names the women, houses them and defines their unfortunate status. Among the women, there is both unity and dissimilarity, 'like an ebony phoenix, each in her own time and with her own season had a story" (TWBP 5).

The representation of the ebony phoenix creates the idea in the beginning that the women rise as from the ashes and prolong to exist. In fact, they struggle throughout their life for a new day and new life. Although the women come to Brewster Place by different and difficult routes, Brewster is a realism that they are, "obliged to share." (Barbara Smith, 1977) Furthermore, with the death of Lorraine and Ben, the women of Brewster Place have become agitated and even Mattie does not sleep well because of her worrying dreams.

Mattie's dream makes her intolerant and uneven for other female inhabitants of Brewster Place, "For all the residents of Brewster Place, an eerie discomfort saturates their existence, hounds their erratic movements, and seeps into their sleep patterns." (Margaret) In Mattie's situation, Naylor uses sleep and dreams as a mean through in which time passes in certainty. In her dream Mattie sees, one after one, all the seven characters in Brewster Place. Mattie and these six characters have faced and tolerated the difficulty, anger, betrayal, male chauvinism and adversity of male humanity. After facing a variety of genres of uncertainty, Mattie dreams and identifies her female characters are equally dependent. The women reveal a sisterhood and show their female relationship. It is a dream that greatly lies and says, "demonic imagery." (Northrop Frye)

Naylor never stops to insist that her characters are answerable in great part for their fortune and their wealth. No one forced Theresa and Loraine to shift from Theresa's Linden Hills residence to Brewster Place. They made the decision to move because their neighbors at Linden Hills had disliked their lesbian relationship and had thus distress Lorraine. Likewise, Mattie Michael could have resided forever in Miss Eva's house but for her mistake in bringing her son up. No one compelled Etta Mae to make her way more than thousand miles from odyssey to Brewster Place, and none have asked Cora Lee to have baby after baby. Against the desires of her parents, Kiswana freely chose to live in a place like Brewster as it was according to her standards.

Like other contemporary African American women writers, Naylor has the beauty of instructing her reader to accept the strength of her characters in the novel as narrated by them. It is easy for Naylor to create a rapport between the reader and her narrator. While her characters are not of an advance class in culture, nor they are mainly learned or well educated, and being unable to boast of either outstanding talents or extraordinary experiences, it is by fairly unusual methods that Naylor obtains a compassionate hearing for her poor characters. From the first chapter, Naylor has selected to break with the custom of having a single and tragic heroine. The attraction of a Mattie lies in the openness of such a character's quality. In her communications with others, her secret trust and fears, her bighearted and calling nature, Mattie exhibits strength of rationale, reliability, good background and a dedicated sense of responsibility. All this would sufficiently qualify her as a worthy character. Naylor recognizes the worldwide quality of women's lives in The Women of Brewster Place,

"The young black woman and the old yellow woman sat in the kitchen for hours, blending their lives so that what lay behind one and ahead of the other became indistinguishable" (TWBP 34).

The African-Americans in Brewster Place are the last of its inhabitants, "...fond of its colored daughters they milled like determined spirits among its decay, trying to make it a home" (TWBP 4). Naylor was making her summit in the last line of her dawn passages,

"they came, they went, grew up, and grew old beyond their years" (TWBP 5).

The inhabitants of Brewster Place particularly the women usually appear to have only the remains and scraps of the greater society. Naylor's comedy in The Women of Brewster Place is both a reflection of their lifestyle and representation of her artistic narrative technique.

The residents of Brewster Place are constantly searching for a home, both as a literal place to live and as a metaphorical state of mind. For Mattie, her search for a home other than the one in which she was raised takes her from a rundown apartment in the city to a wonderful home in which she raises her child, and finally, to Brewster Place. The journey from one home to another is repeated with every character in the novel. Just as important as any physical location is the security and comfort attached to the idea of home. Brewster Place, though it's falling apart, offers Etta a form of security and comfort she has long lived without. It offers Kiswana the opportunity to live out her ideals, and it offers Mattie the opportunity to become a surrogate mother to a host of women. In every search for a home, what ultimately defines the idea of "home" isn't the condition of the walls but the strength of the relationships within those walls.

The residents have migrated to Brewster Place from their parents' home in the South, from the Mediterranean, from the middle-class suburbs ringing the city, or from more secure lives and homes. Regardless of where they come from, they have ended up here, and they have chosen, or been forced, to call it home. Migration, in addition to being a central theme of the novel, is also a central theme in Afro American history. From the slave migration to the North prior to the Civil War, to the Great Migration of millions of Afro Americans following the post-World War II industrial boom, the idea of escaping to the North has always held hope and promise of a better future.

For most of the residents of Brewster Place, however, migration isn't the fulfillment of a dream but the culmination of a long, frustrating life. Mattie loses her home and ends up in Brewster Place, while Etta arrives after a series of failed relationships. Ben comes to Brewster Place after being abandoned by his wife and daughter, while Lorraine and Theresa are forced out of their more comfortable middle-class existence because of their sexuality. Despite the frustrations and difficulties of life in Brewster Place, it brings all of its residents hope, a light is left on all night, a late-night conversation brings comfort, and many of those searching for meaning find some version of it here.

Gloria has a strong consequence on her characters and the location of the novel. Seven women of different backgrounds face sensitive hardships and difficulties under different conditions before reaching to Brewster Place. The setting of the novel is the wall of Brewster Place, a dead- end street and is also a symbol of triple jeopardy which is being continually faced by the Black women. The novel has seven short stories and each story focuses on different woman characters, which experience and accept disputes of male dominated people, where the males torture and disgrace the women by various means. But these women accept the disgrace with courage and strength of mind. One of the most important features of the novel is committed to the racial and sexual domination and bearing of these nuisances, the women strives hard to survive in the oppressive society with a feel of affection. In this place, the novelist represents these aspects through the characters of Mattie, Etta Mea, Kiswana, Lucielia and Lorraine

The women of Brewster Place was meant to celebrate the female spirit and the ability to transcend and also to give a microcosm of black women in America- Black women who are faced by a wall of racism and sexism. (Pearl Cleage, 57)

Naylor portrays the depressed conditions of her character step by step and in this string, Mattie a protagonist suffers the hurting of rape and unwanted pregnancy. It is unlucky that her own community's man rapes her and her father treats her roughly. At last, Mattie leaves her family and goes to live out of Brewster Place. Mattie's great courage motivates Etta to gain confidence in facing darker times. Out of the seven characters in the novel, only Etta who apparently rejects the white's order and implies her female heroism against male chauvinism. Etta is another case of rape prey. She was entirely tricked by Reverend Moreland Wood, who very shrewdly confuses her and spoils her virginity. After destroying, she comes to Mattie and Mattie responds as a true friend. Kiswana is novel's another example of female heroism in this novel. It is her heroism that she deliberately rejects her own name 'Melanie' into African name 'Kiswana'. She continually faces her mother's dissatisfaction but in spite of it, she does things which yield her a kind of recognition in black society.

Mattie, Etta and Kiswana, are other examples of female heroism. She is looked after by Mattie and finally settles down with Eugene. When their daughter gets electrocuted and after Serena's death, Ciel becomes detached but it was Mattie, who relieves her from the stress as a mother and gets her back to self-confidence. Mattie being a sign of female heroism takes power in everything and it was due her hard work that once again Ciel starts her life with new willpower. At last, both women being mutual reliant, show their female heroism against stubborn and inflexible conditions. Naylor uses lesbian relationship in her novel because she wants to show her female characters are brave and courageous in the male dominated society. Being homosexual, both women face and experience the harmful approach of the culture. Before the rape incident the people of Brewster Place had discarded the lesbians but after the rape episode, the total community wants to take action against the rapists. Though Lorraine dies but her existence does not die in the minds of people.

Throughout the novel, characters reach out to one another across generational, cultural, and gender lines. They reach out to one another and in doing so, they are able to ease the loneliness and hardship that surround their lives. One example of a powerful personal connection is Mattie's relationship with Eva. The women are separated by class, skin tone, and age, yet they find each other and make each other's lives more bearable. Similar benefits arise from other connections, including Mattie's relationship with Etta, Mattie's relationship with Lucielia, Kiswana's relationship with Cora, and Ben's relationship with Lorraine. Each relationship shows how personal connections can sustain and offer hope in even the direst circumstances. The relationships show individuals at their best, and they serve as a necessary counterweight to the abandonment, prejudice, and brutality that comprise much of the novel.

In Brewster Place, births are nearly always illegitimate. Every child we hear about is missing a father, from Mattie's son to all of Cora's children. These children are missing half their identities, and their fates seem terrible, just as the fate of Brewster Place itself seems dire. Brewster Place's conception is even referred to as a bastard birth. From the moment of Brewster Place's creation, its fate is sealed, the buildings and their inhabitants destined to live in ever-worsening conditions.

The men in The Women of Brewster Place are masters at disappearing, faced with any hardship or difficulty, men such as Basil, Eugene, and Butch run from any responsibility. Their flight is in direct response to any perceived threat to their freedom. Basil disappears when faced with the remote possibility of going to jail. Eugene disappears once his responsibilities as a father and husband become too demanding, and Butch Fuller lives a philosophy dedicated to living in the moment. While the men in the novel are constantly running away, the women are constantly returning home to one another.

The wall separating Brewster Place from the main avenues of the city serves several important purposes. Following its initial creation, the wall comes to symbolize the indifference with which Brewster Place is treated by the men responsible for its creation. Because of the wall, Brewster Place is economically and culturally isolated from the rest of the city. The wall has forced Brewster Place to be a fend for itself. For the residents of Brewster Place, the wall symbolizes the fact that for most of them, Brewster Place will be the end of the road. Their lives will go no further, regardless of how much they may hope or dream. The wall, for them, represents the wall that has been built around their lives, either by failed opportunities or by a series of misfortunes. The true disastrousness of the wall becomes evident at the end of the novel. Along this wall, Lorraine drags her nearly lifeless body after she is gang raped, and it is from this wall that she grabs the brick and she uses that to kill Ben.

The novel encloses that the women of Brewster Place tolerate and experience the domination of black and white people. These people are vigorous and strong wall of Brewster Place against all kinds of dominance. They succeed in constructing a new black community which has become a sturdy, power, confident and strong-minded to the white society. Within this new community and relationship, the people of Brewster Place can live with their own requirements and endurance with respect. They make their own rules and laws stand by all. Nobody can challenge and disgrace them.

Although Brewster Place is a symbol of dehumanization and effort but however, these seven women come out of this suffering and try to dwell their life on their own way. The breathing place as a 'dead-end-street' becomes a painful and dictatorial place for the seven characters of Naylor. The wall of control in Brewster Place always separates blacks from white community, so to eliminate the separation between white and black, the women devastate and breach the wall of Brewster Place. The wall is the dismal and main sign of lower quality and partiality towards the colored people. By means of breaking the wall, the women's first effort stops but is not yet completed.

The novel ends with the "Dusk". The Brewster Place has been condemned and deserted in the end, As Naylor states,

But the colored daughter of Brewster, spread over the canvas of time, still wake up with their dreams misted on the edge of a yawn. They get up and pin those dreams to wet laundry hung out to dry, they're diapered around babies. They ebb and flow, ebb and flow, but never disappear. (TWBP 192)

Naylor's humor is usually an added naive and open-hearted selection. For example, there is hot friendship in the humor of the justification by Etta Mae of her stealing the car, a humor not openly at anyone's cost, but based on undeclared, shared acceptance between the two friends. Certainly, many of the interactions between Mattie and Etta are mocking and humorous. The subsequent lines from the novel express the above context,

My, my, you the most impatient Christian I know. Probably the only Christian you know. You plan on dazzling the Lord, Etta? Well, honey, last I heard. He wasn't available. You got more recent news? (TWBP 62).

It is a pleasant humor, entirely canceled of hatred or other darker feeling. This is all more amazing because when seen in circumstance, Mattie's warning, her criticism of Etta's improper dressing, and Etta's playfulness, disrespectful reply. Though aware that they are half-playing certain roles - Mattie as the good Christian woman and Etta as the teasing one - the two friends are able to speak their minds and make their stand with expressiveness. There is an apparent tendency of social and domestic fighting in The Women of Brewster Place, a style which is more common in the working course.

A patriarchal society is the model in this novel. Patriarchal community may not directly allow domestic cruelty, but they are rarely framed to stop it from incidence. When order is endangered or broken down in a patriarchal society, women are usually the first to be punished. Sticking badly onto the shreds of their self-esteem, some men give way to their baser character. However, it must be noted that there is a marked difference between the varieties of patriarchy experienced in Brewster Place. In the African American tradition as revealed in The Women of Brewster Place, the women imagine more than their men, as they strive to accomplish their roles as thoughtful wives and good mothers as a sign to grasp the rights expecting monetary support and emotional loyalty from their partners.

Some women however in the African American society command respect and receive it, even from the most unwilling men. For example, Eugene even resents her, and in his anger, he is vulgar to her, but he does not dare refuse her doorway into his residence. It may even be against his force, but he has a firm respect for her. Writing as she did in the early 1980s, Naylor consciously "bent over backwards not to have a negative message come through about the men" (Southern Review 576). When Sam Michael beats his daughter, he is still painted in shades of grey, and he is still a character one could pity - his anger was awaken by his dejected feelings of disloyalty in his love of his daughter. "Sam Michael looked at it, saw it was his daughter, and he dropped the stick and wept" (TWBP 24). Naylor quickly guides the reader away from dwelling on this by having Mattie remember her father without accusation whenever she thinks of him. When Sam Michael weeps, Ben mourns his daughter, they are converted because they lament. They are not hermits, but their regret converts them from being lost spirit. Naylor may have desire to prevent an extensive negative of men in her novel.

Through a concerned portrayal of the sufferings of some women, Naylor displays that men like Butch, Basil, Eugene and the others are fading their women when they are careless, overly needy or gutless. Naylor does grant that there are cases where no pardon is possible, but on the intact, it can be seen that with the passage of time, Naylor bends over backwards further and further to ensure a least of negativity in her representation of male characters. In Mattie's dream, all these women take part to destroy the wall, demolishing through the barricade that cut them off from potential. The book's epigraph is the last line of Langston Hughes' poem, "Or does explode?" is recognized in violently graphic representation.

The answer is an echoing "Yes." But to explode is not to be broken. These black women, "as a community, will vary their dreams into another day. When Mattie wakes from this dream, the sun is shining."(TWBP 12) These stories are joined by more than the life on which the characters live. The communications of the characters and the similar efforts they live during connect the stories, as do the persistent themes and motifs. Of these combining essentials, the most notable is the dream pattern, for though these women live a dreadful existence, they are united by their common dreams. In all these women, individual identity is shaped within the template of a community. The Women of Brewster Place tells the tales of the working class Afro American society.

Brewster Place is full of colour, from the clothes the children wear on a summer afternoon to the colour of its residents. Naylor describes the colour of nearly every character that appears in the novel. Characters are described as caramel, honey, light-skinned, dark-skinned, and blue-eyed. In describing characters this way, Naylor shows the spectrum of shades and experiences that have defined African-American culture. There is a diversity of experiences, evident not only in the lives of the characters but in the characters' very skin. In addition, the colour of the residents also occasionally serves as a contrast to the drab colours that otherwise characterize Brewster Place. The sky may be gray and the walls "ashen," but the residents of Brewster Place, full of life, are vibrant and rich.

Conclusion

At the close of this novel, there are few optimistic transformations taking place. Cora Lee persists to have one baby after another, Etta Mae and Mattie finds no way to leave Brewster Place, Loraine is no more, Theresa leaves the place. The lack of any changes or victories won is by no means an unenthusiastic departure letter from the author. The women in Naylor's first novel do not have fairytale endings of ideal lives but neither are they crushed by their very defective ones. They will not live happily always, but they live on. By her close attention to the most trifling of details in their lives, by giving her characters a voice, Naylor's intention could not have been apparent - namely that in the very endurance of her normal characters in such a world as they find themselves dwelling in, Naylor observes reason to rejoice. They survive by developing and maintaining enthusiasm, dedication and flexibility. The victory of the Brewster Place women is a discreet one, a victory which lies not in conquering marvelous odds, but in organizing to endure them. It ends,

"They ebb and flow, ebb and flow, but never disappear" (TWBP 192).

CHAPTER FOUR

Linden Hills: Chauvinistic Relations and Reflection on Female Black Identity

"They all trying to say something with music that you can't say with plain talk. There ain't really no words for love or pain. And the way I see it, only fools go around trying to talk their love or talk their pain. So the smart people make music and you can kinda hear about it without them saying anything."

--- Gloria Naylor, *Linden Hills*

Introduction

Linden Hills is the best example of artistic creation of racism in a Black society. Naylor makes frequent use of the cinematic code of editing in order to focus the attention of the reader on some particular point in the narrative. Faulkner says, "The setting of *Linden Hills* makes it clear that Naylor is creating a geographical fictional world". Naylor establishes two dissimilar communities rich and poor, beside each other for a closer understanding of the whole Black community. The geographical setting of the novel as well as the shape of the place on map makes the covered realities of the Black community perceptible to the human eye. The "V-shape allows his land to be both self-enclosed yet situated in the world. And since Nedeed lives on the lowest level of 'the hills,' he stands as a sentry to his private development" (Christian 109). Naylor had adapted Dante's *Inferno* to her own fictional purposes, in this instance a tale of lost black souls trapped in the American dream" (Christian 109). At the bottom of Linden Hills where the most opulent homes are, "...the seat of the successive generations of the dark "satanic Luther Nedeed" (Sherley Anne 10). The original Luther was freedman, who has bought the land in the 1820's rented shacks to blacks who were too poor to farm.

Artistic Characters of the Novel

The novel title deals with the lives of wealthy African Americans who have attained the American Dream of material achievement at the outlay of humanistic morals. Naylor is primarily concerned with female characters, and although the plight of black women is not ignored in this novel. In this novel the hero Luther Nedeed, the male chauvinist, even though he has a very good economic background blindly follows his ancestors and avenges white women without even discovering the truth. All the minor characters who support Luther try to pretend as if they are well mannered and descent, but the fact is different which we can discover through their life style. Though the coloured Americans have freedom to live, and wealth to prosper they fail to enjoy, because of the dependence they have in their unconscious mind. They are unsuccessful in keeping up their potential and unknowingly they fall a prey into others hands. They cheat themselves and they fail to be independent because of their inborn anxiety.

Nedeed himself, a sufferer of the racist Whites, founded Linden Hills to be a shelter and a paradise to Black people however, it comes to be a means of exploiting Black people. Linden Hills is unique because the people who live there have grown out of the greed, and they pay attention to the diabolic intellect and they were guarded by the brutal will power of Luther's successors. Nedeed had built these wooden shacks up on the hill and rented them out to local blacks who are too poor to farm and earn their living from the saw-mills and tar pit. He also wants to rent out shacks along with the tupelo Drive, but no one wants to dwell in the part of cemetery land, so the local blacks loudly rebuff. Luther goes away for a while in the spring of 1837 and brings back an octoroon wife. She is about twenty years old and Nedeed had owned Linden Hills for almost seventeen years by then. She gives him a son the following winter, who is, "...short, squat, dark, and with an immobile face, even from birth" (LH 4).

Luther leaves his land and the business to send this only son to the fancy boarding schools for his bright future and to hold on to worthless hill land. But the son comes back to the land and holds his father's property and business on his quite back. When old Luther dies in 1879, actually old Luther does not die because his son, too, brings an "octoroon" woman into his home as a wife, Willa Prescott, who gives birth to another Luther Nedeed. Nothing is changing in the bottom of Linden hills. There is another generation of big frog and little frog going through the hills together every first of the month to collect rent. Old Luther's son is finally able to rent shacks along Tupelo Drive. The tenants rebuffed before and now, they don't seem to mind that they are surrounded by a cemetery. The dwellers of Linden Hills are very poor and they paid their rent so long as they did it promptly on the first of the month. But Nedeed starts to collect the high charges of huts on the first of the month. He does not care about their feeling on paying their rent. Finding no substitute, the poor inhabitants start to reside in the same place and keep paying him rent for that same place and letting him bury their dead. And as the faces on the hill changed and the old town becomes a young city. Needed watches the development of the place and sitting on his porch watches the sun as, "...it always had over his world" (LH 6). Linden Hills will prove it. Luther has given his people some of the most expensive property in the county. They have the land for a millennium. Now just let them sit on it and do what they do best. Luther separates himself from his people by his values, as well as by the artificial lake which is really a moat he built around his house and grounds.

At the same time, Nedeed wants to get rid of the unwanted tenants by either buying or tricking them out of their leases. He finally manages to clear out most of the upper slope. When he reaches 'First Crescent Drive', he faces a trouble with Grandmother

Tilson, a resident in first crescent drive. She completely rejects his plan because she used to fish with Luther's father in this artificial pond and he had given this ground to her and, so she is not interested to give it to him. Though Needed does not live longer, he visualizes the outlines of his place crystallized into a zoned district of eight circular drives that held some of the finest homes for the wealthiest black families in the country. Linden Hills is a place where people work hard and save hard for the privilege to rest in the soft shadows of heart shaped tress. The Tupelo Drive and Luther Nedeed became one cry of dark victory for blacks outside and inside Linden Hills.

Willie and Lester start their journey downward in Linden Hills. The black boy Willie whom people used to call white Willie grew up in the Putney Wayne, bordering place of Linden Hills and, Lester has the colour of a baby's shit whom people call shit born and raised in Linden Hills. They are very close friends, they had been inseparable in junior high school, and it is there they have picked up their nicknames and their desires to be poets. Willie and Lester approach each other on the side of the school yard. After junior high school and almost after a long time, they again meet each other. Both had graduated, Lester to Spring Vale High school and Willie to the streets, due to some family problems he passes his life on the streets writing poems. Willie had left school after the ninth grade. Lester's mother always wants to send him in University. So Lester goes up to university and then takes a graduation degree only because of his mother Tilson's hard work.

Lester then joins Willie in giving poetry readings in coffeehouses, bookstores, and the city park. They support themselves with odd jobs because they cannot make a living from their work. Willie is almost twenty years old. He has the habit of creating stanzas in his mind and eventually had a repertoire in the hundreds. He became familiar on Wayne Avenue by seeking out fewer jobs over the year. He gains the respect of Wayne Avenue because "... he is a deep dude" (LH 29) so rents a room in Wayne county and starts to drink and smoke with young black men who are either tired of looking for work or tired of finding it.

Norman and Ruth, "...an exemplary model of a happily married couple; it is significant that they make their home outside of Linden Hills" (Whitt, op.cit., 73).

The married couple Ruth and Norman is old friend of Willie and Lester. Willie is always awed in front of Ruth but often he dreams about her. Both the friends crossed the Linden Hills and enter into Norman Anderson's dilapidated garden in which apartment buildings are being constructed. Norman often goes to hospital and comes out after three months because he suffers from some mental problem. He cannot keep a job for more than a year and nine months. He comes out of the hospital after three months and usually gets a new job within a week, or at the most two. But then a year and nine months later, it will happen again. Ruth as a woman who wants children comes to know that Norman cannot fulfill her desire. Ruth is completely tired, of hurting from being crushed between her hatred and love of her husband.

Meanwhile Roxanne enters the home, who is the statistical proof that black men are further behind white men than ever before. She is so passionate that she pays her dues to the civil right movement and enrolls her name in the black history course in college. During the conversation Mrs. Tilson set the dining room table with china, silver - ware, and linen napkins in honour of Willie. Roxanne, Lester's sister, a hypocrite who wants to settle in life by marry well. She dominates the conversation with the importance of her new promotion and mention Xavier's name for sixth time, Lester gets angry and throws the chicken thigh bone he is sucking because he hates him. Roxanne flushes deeply and says, "Xavier is the vice president of minority marketing at General Motors, and what have you done except scrape a plate clean" (LH 55). Being insulted in front of his friend, Lester immediately answers her that he has done plenty and working for immortality. On hearing the word 'immortality' she sarcastically says that writing crap is not a job, they are really your junk. Lester calls Willie and leaves the place. He follows Lester up the stairs. Willie sits at the edge of the bed and starts to narrate Lester about his family that he grew up with five brothers and sisters in three rooms, three small rooms and his mom got beaten by his father every day. Willie is discouraged by his family's condition and feels pity towards his family.

Lester and Willie, in the name of the waiters they are hired to clear the trash and to clean the dishes. They join the marriage ceremony and feel surprised to take part in that congregation of high and mighty black people's classy party. Xavier Donnell attends the marriage ceremony, during the ceremony his activities make Lester to get angry with him. Xavier is almost thirty-one years old, who is the lover of Lester's sister, with the post of vice president of minority marketing at General Motors. He is a man of high principles but in Roxanne's case, he is confused in selecting her as his choice. He gets advice about marrying Roxanne from his senior Maxwell Smyth, who is an executive at General Motors. Maxwell advises against it because, "That family has one foot in the ghetto and the other on a watermelon rind" (LH 116). In the marriage hall Xavier sits with a young yellow woman and enjoys giving her cheese and whispers in her ears they laugh. On seeing these, Lester decides to talk about him to Roxanne and takes revenge against him.

Two friends have started their new job of shoveling the snow from Mrs. Dumont's house. Laurel Dumont, who is the wife of Mr. Howard Dumont the first black D.A. in Wayne County, chooses her career as an IBM executive instead of music and swimming. After the death of Laurel's mother, her father remarries, and then she spends most of her days with her grandmother Roberta Johnson in Georgia. As she grows up, she graduates Phi Beta Kappa from Berkeley and works her way into a top executive position at IBM.

Though Laurel marries a successful person, she remains distant from her husband. She destroys her inner self in order to be successful and free, which leads to divorce. Actually the land was only leased to the Dumont's in 1903, so Luther Nedeed wants to vacate his house from Laurel Dumont because Luther comes to know that Mr. Howard Dumont is leaving the house and his wife Laurel in Tupelo Drive. In her confrontation with Luther, who makes her mentally very weak, she wears her bathing suit and dives off the high board into the twenty-foot end of an empty swimming pool. This suicide is not considered as a cowardly act by James Robert Saunders, he says in portraying Laurel, Naylor builds on the feminist statement that Laurel is indeed trapped in a life dictated by her husband's social position and standards perpetuated by Linden Hills. Willie is shocked by Laurel's suicide. In the meantime, another old witness desires to know more about the suicide.

Professor Daniel Braithwaite is a history scholar whose education has been aided by Nedeed. He settled down in Linden Hills after receiving his Doctorate. As a retired history professor, his life's work has been recording the history of Linden Hills. Lester asks Braithwaite that laurel was crazy to commit suicide but he insists that she was insane and true insanity which caused her death. With all his knowledge Professor Daniel Braithwaite has written a twelve-volume history of Linden Hills. Braithwaite is doubtful about Laurel's suicide that somebody might have killed Laurel or reason for her suicide. He draws the attention of two friends towards Nedeed. Teresa Goddu says "by focusing on Luther's individual achievement rather than the collective accomplishments of Linden Hills, Braithwaite transforms a communal history into the myth of a single, 'special' man." Braithwaite instead being against the activities of Luther, simply he replicates Luther's description of Linden Hills.

Next Willa discovers the history of Nedeed's another wife, Priscilla McGuire, who had an animated character portrayed by Naylor. Her history is brought forth by a series of photographs represent her gradual change to a fading personality in her own life. She changes from a passionate woman with a strong sense of her own identity to a finding and finally her presence disappears. In the last photo, she is found to blot out her face and in the empty space a word me was written by Priscilla. As Willa begins to look at one of her predecessors in the family photo album, she observes progression of a woman who literally fades disappears from the photograph:

"Her face was gone. The photo album trembled in her cold hands as she realized there was no mistaking what she now saw: Priscilla McGuire ended at the neck and without her features,... She came to the last photograph, And scrawled across the empty hole in lilac-coloured ink was the word me (LH 249)

Naylor sketches Willa's fear that she too has to face the same fate for herself. First Luwana, then Evelyn, and then Priscilla are intently erased from the Luther family for three generations, so Willa plans to find a way out of her cellar imprisonment. Willa slowly becomes conscious of her own condition. In an interview with Toni Morrison Naylor states that,

I created a way for her to see her own reflection in a pail of water because she had no self until the moment. And when she realized that she had a face, then maybe she had other things going for her as well. And she could take her destiny in her own hands. (An Interview with Toni Morrison - 78)

Laurel Dumont and Priscilla McGuire had never met, but they are mystically linked through the dreadfulness of Willie and Willa, their horror an indication of the depth of emotion evoked in them at the resulting plight of these women, a horror born of natural concern which Laurel and Priscilla, for whatever reasons, did not receive in their lifetimes.

It is the easiest means of identification to say this was the Luther who married Luwana Packerville, or Evelyn Creton, or Priscilla McGuire, or Willa Prescott. Without the names which are maiden names, and personalities of their wives, it would seem that all the Luthers were one. Living in the same house with the same ambitions and habits, were it possible for the four Mrs. Nedeeds ever to meet and compare experiences, it is likely they would be a witness to being effectively married to one and the same man. The Luthers seem happy to carry on their tradition of always being "Luther Nedeed" as they each try to shape their wives to fit the shape of the self-effacing and effaced Mrs. Nedeed, and nothing else.

The similarity of all the generations of Luthers is the secret of the Nedeed strength and prosperity. Loyal adherence to tradition is what enables each Nedeed to flourish. The fifth Luther Nedeed came to his terrible end, burning to death as if in the fire of hell, because he had broken with two vital traditions of his forefathers. Firstly, he had failed to bring a pale-skinned bride into his house who would be flexible and would ensure the sequence of his family. It would seem that for a Nedeed, a break in tradition is indeed fatal. Even an innocent transgressing of tradition does not go unpunished. The sixth and unacknowledged Nedeed, who is Sinclair Nedeed, broke with tradition, albeit not through any fault of his own, by being pale skinned instead of black skin, and this caused his father to reject the child and kill him by locking him in a basement. As he did not bear the name of Luther, he did not have the chance to be a Nedeed and to flourish as his ancestors had done.

The fifth Luther Nedeed moves through the novel bringing despair and darkness into the lives of those he touches, an antithesis to a character like Ruth who brings renewed hope to all who come in contact with her. It is implicit in the plot of the novel that Luther's is the hidden hand behind the marriage of Winston Alcott, separating him from the person dearest to him. Nedeed was aware that Laurel Dumont would soon commit suicide because he had a hand in driving her to that state. Like the essence of evil, Nedeed commits the entire range of sins which damn people down into the City of Non – violence against his wife and neighbours, and against the natural state of things, fraudulence and manipulation of others in his power to devastating ends, provoking the despairing to self-violence, and committing the canonical sin of disloyalty, betraying his son, his tenants, and all who look to him for guidance.

The male character in the novel who comes closest to attaining an understanding of women and their psyche is Willie. No one apart from Willie had realized the disappearance of Willa. The smoothness of Luther's explanations disguises the truth as easily as the store-bought cake he brought to the wake had disguised his lies. It was only Willie who was puzzled by the discrepancy, "the way the butter, rum and raisins went down all smooth and easy he had almost missed tasting her absence" (LH 147). Willie is not typical of a conventionally masculine man. There are hints in the novel of his homosexual tendencies, tendencies thus far unindulged, and these tendencies seem to enable him to comprehend from a feminine perspective. Lester, who is less sensitive than Willie, goes through Linden Hills undisturbed and untroubled by dreams in his sleeping hours, "I am gone before my head hits the pillow" (LH 211). At the marriage reception, it is only the three men who have homosexual tendencies, Willie, Winston and David, who understand the Whitman poem. There appears to be an understated point here that those who are at the furthest ends of the scales of manliness and femininity are those furthest from reaching an understanding of one another.

What the Nedeed women had not known was that like their husbands, they lost strength when they lost their tradition, even if it was a tradition no one had yet cherished. Laurel Dumont failed to listen to the wisdom of her grandmother, Roberta, and failed to find a solution to her problems, just as Mrs. Tilson, paying no notice to the teaching of Mamie Tilson, tries to rush her son and daughter further down Linden Hills, not knowing that she would be rushing them to their devastation. Mrs. Tilson appears in the light of a self-deluding woman, but one with a certain amount of manipulative power in her home. The Linden Hills women are generally thought to be rather privileged women of the middle or upper-middle classes. Roxanne, Willa, Laurel, not one of them seem to have found peace or happiness. The only woman in *Linden Hills* who is a happy woman is Ruth Anderson who had once lived in Linden Hills, but now lives in Putney Wayne and would never consent to returning to Linden Hills because she treasures her happiness.

The predicament of Willa Prescott Nedeed represents the circumstances under which all the needed wives met with their end. Willa Nedeed is a symbol of sufferings at the hands of her husband. Like other preceding Nedeed women, Willa's story ends in, "progressive depersonalization" (Ranveer 130). Willa has been put into the basement by her husband, Luther, who is the last in a long line of Nedeed men. Willa's offense is merely that she bore a child with light-skin. In presenting the Nedeed dynasty, Naylor has presented another extreme case of male oppression and as in the case of women in Brewster Place, one can understand the limits, Nedeed women bear the pain for their own plights. It is Willa herself, who wanted to be a Nedeed woman. Her husband's distant ancestor was the founder of Linden Hills and the Nedeeds have always handled considerable power. Although she has been transferred to the basement, the will to emerge out of it, still remains in Willa's hands.

During the discourse with Toni Morrison, Naylor reveals that "Willa's end is the appropriate climax of the novel and through the end of Willa's character; she i.e. [Willa]" gains the appreciation as well as sympathy and consolation from everyone. From the starting of the novel, Willa is only one black woman, belonging to Nedeed family, who does not care about the rules and perceives of this family and after facing enough remarkable problems, she presents her real existence. In the climax of the novel, Willie and Lester, residents of

Linden Hills, observe each and every incident and come to the conclusion about Willa that she was a venturesome spirit. People just watch the burning of the Nedeed house and do not attempt to help them out.

In this series we can see another example of Laurel Dumont. She has been a winner all her life, "To attain the present level, she has to cultivate her natural and physical talents though she starved emotionally" (Ranveer 126). Laurel too throughout the life faces such adversities which are given by her father as well as her husband. When she was quiet young, her mother dies and her father remarries and as a result, she feels alienated by her stepmother. With the passage of time, she grows up and after graduation; she works and finally marries Howard Dumont. But the harmony between the couple breaks soon and she remains emotionally separated from her husband. As a result, Mr. Dumont decides to divorce her, which makes her enraged. Laurel Dumont too is the victim of torment and exile. Although she does not bear physical violence yet she suffers from mental agony. She gradually becomes mentally disturbed and as she meets Mr. Nedeed, he makes her realize that there is no inner core to her person but only a frightening void (Ranveer126).

Another character Cassandra who is rarely mentioned in the novel, is made the victim of another, "spurious marriage" (Ranveer 129) with the homosexual Winston Alcott, who betrays himself and his male lover David for responsibility as an attorney. Cassandra faces deceive and torments by her husband. Despite being a homosexual, Winston deliberately marries with Cassandra deceiving her about his homosexuality. Cassandra as a dutiful wife does not cross her limitation but after bearing a lot of pressure, she finally recognizes her identity and decides to confront her husband boldly. There are some male characters in the novel, who bear the same conditions and after much resistance, they too come up by giving rebirth to their identity and dignity. In this connection, the first two characters come in the mind are Willie and Lester, who are good friends. They have faced adversity as well as ill-will in the society.

Naylor lets the character learn and live in her own way, thus showing that as Willa's author and creator, she is the first who must learn to respect the principles Willa chooses for herself. It is not by cutting down her husband's individuality that Willa assumes an individuality of her own. Her lack of desire for revenge is her way of showing that she is strong enough to wrestle an identity for herself without infringing on that of others. Christine G. Berg in her essay, "Light from a hill of carbon paper dolls", explains the probable causes of Naylor for getting inspiration to do her creative work. Naylor's use of the Inferno functions in several key ways. It provides a canvas upon which she can draw the details of her contemporary Hell.

Naylor celebrates the strength of Willa by showing that her heroine is no longer afraid to choose a course of action she deems holds happiness for her, even if it overlaps with what has been stereotyped as unbecoming submissiveness. Willa does not simply negate a male assertion of her identity, but ends with creating a new definition of herself, even if that does mean including elements criticized by others. With the full knowledge of the wrongs of all the former Mrs. Nedeeds and her own wrongs, Willa accepts the past and prepares to pick up her life from the present point and no other.

Plot: The Infernal Bough

Most of the critics claim that *Linden Hills* is a modern version of Dante's Inferno "in which souls are damned not because they have offended God or have violated a religious system but because they have offended themselves". The setting of Linden Hills is actually not several hills but only part of one hillside-a large, V-shaped area intersected by eight streets that curve around and down the slope. Linden Hills consist of eight concentric drives. Naylor portrays America's middle class blacks who are living on First Crescent Drive through to Fifth Crescent Drive and upper middle class blacks, who are living on Tupelo Drive, the street on which no one can turn around - representation of the Dungeon of Dis, the abode of Satan, in Dante's Inferno. A story in the search of money and authority is the innermost subject in it. Therefore, they have often idealized another solution in their search for liberty.

The novel begins with an introductory chapter and is then divided into sections identified by date, from December 19 to December 24. It is the story of four days journey by the two protagonists Willie K Mason and Willa Prescott Nedeed. Willie has a physical journey moving down the hill, communicating with different peoples, a journey that begins for finding a job but ends in his maturity and a full-developed way of thinking on Blacks especially Black women. The novel narrates the happenings and occurrences that two young Black poets undertake in their trip from the lower class Putney Wayne to the middle class section of

Linden Hills. Willie K Mason and Lester Tilson two contemporary young Black poets decide to find a job a few days before Christmas in the wealthy community of Linden Hills to buy gifts for their families. On the other hand, Willa's journey is an emotional and a mental journey into the past. This journey also results in self-actualization and resisting the dominance and oppression of the Black patriarchy.

The setting is Linden Hills and an upper middle-class black community built on a huge plot of land owned by the mysterious Nedeed family. Luther Nedeed, who founded Linden Hills and its community, has a frightening history. After the first Luther Nedeed, each subsequent generation has son named Luther who looks exactly like his father. Likewise, each generation marries a light skinned woman who is immediately absorbed into the identity of Mrs. Nedeed. However, these wives are not allowed to mix freely with other families and, "...it reflects the life of all the residents of Linden Hills" (Kashinath Ranveer, 1995). Linden Hills' proprietors, the satanic Luther Nedeeds are the most damned people of Gloria Naylor's Hell. Nedeeds control all the circles of V – shaped Linden Hills from bottom to the top as Satan did in inferno. They commit numerous sins both to themselves and their families and to their own people.

The first chapter explains the history of the Nedeed family. Luther Nedeed, an ancestor of the current character, bought Linden Hills from its white owners during the period prior to the American civil war. It was accessible for sale because the white owners measured the hills unsuitable for farming. And the entire bottom of the hill is hemmed in by the town cemetery, Nedeed became an undertaker. Naylor has created a critical portrait of a "perverted Eden" (Ward 12), in which the upper middle class has achieved material success at the cost of their identity. The male dominants are physically healthy, but spiritually and culturally malnutritioned. He built shacks on the hills and rented them to local black families.

He then went to Mississippi and brought back an octoroon wife, Luwana Packerville, who delivered a son and brought him up to take over his father's name, looks, and business. Once the government and real estate developers wanted his land so badly, he decided to insure that they would never be able to get their hands on it. So the second Nedeed sold the land practically for air to the blacks who are shacking there. He gave them a lease of a thousand years and a day. The lease also provided that they pass their property to their children. And if they wanted to sell it, they had to sell it to another black family or the rights would revert back to the Nedeeds. The Tupelo Realty Corporation holds the mortgages and leases on all the residences in Linden Hills, which the new Tupelo Realty Company financed, constructed, and sell' the private developments, and Nedeed is the accountable for the African American community. He lives at the bottom of the slope. The most affluent families live at the bottom of the hill, while the less affluent live at the top.

Luther's double great- grandfather who came from Mississippi buys the entire northern area of the plateau and the hilly land, Tupelo Drive. He builds a two-room cabin at the bottom of the slope - the dead centre, and after the cabin is finished, people could see him sitting in front of it for an hour at dawn, high moon, and dusk. He sat every day for exactly seven days with a guess, "he's trying to think a living out of that land." (LH 2) There is something in Luther Nedeed's short, squat body that stopped those white men from treating him like a nigger and even thinking the word negro. He plans about the establishment of Linden Hills because he desires his community to be influential and powerful through materialistic achievements. "But Nedeed didn't try to farm Linden Hills." (LH 2) Always Linden Hills is bounded with certain dealings and disputes but there sustains one fact, never disputed by anyone is that the Nedeeds have always lived there.

Norman has been telling Ruth that soon as we get money, we apply for a house in Linden Hills and you live in it alone but Ruth dislikes this idea because he hates to dwell in Linden Hills and she says those folks just aren't real. Even Lester dislikes the dwellers of Linden Hills and calls them '... a bunch of the saddest niggers'

(LH 39). At the same time the poor Willie is ready to go for work, Lester and Willie reach the Lester's home and Lester makes Willie to stay at his house that night. Mrs. Tilson feels happy to see Willie after a long time but Willie feels inferior and awkward in front of the yellow woman because of his black skin. Though Mrs. Tilson skin is in Yellow colour, she belongs to black society and knows very well about the hardships of the blacks to dwell in front of this white society. Willie has to agree that there is nothing wrong in her knowing. She says that she has to live in this house almost on the charity of other people and lead her life for Lester and Roxanne.

The novel sketches two journeys. The physical journey of Willie K Mason's down the Linden Hills, on the other side Naylor's heroine Willa's journey discovering the history of the Nedeed women and their failures. The clock on the morgue wall ticks for the sixtieth time pas mid-night, the wife of Luther Nedeed, Willa sits at the edge of the cot with her son's head resting on her shoulder. She knows very well that the days are gone, so many are gone. But she waits for the basement door to open by Luther. She believes that Luther will unlock the door since the child is sick. Luther fixes his nightly brandy and soda for it has been a difficult day and the next day will be even busier. He prepares to join the Parker funeral in two days and he must be ready to act as an usher at Winston Alcott's wedding ceremony the next day morning.

The second crescent drive resident of Linden Hills, Winston Alcott is homosexual resident, breaks his eight years relationship with his gay lover David to get married and to stop the rumour about him. As the president of the Tupelo Reality Corporation and as an old friend of the Alcott, Luther Nedeed grants him a mortgage on Tupelo Drive for his dedication and loyalty to Luther. Lester and Willie make themselves clear that this marriage party is going to be a sophisticated one, so there will not be any place for blacks. David comes to attend the marriage ceremony and says to Winston that, "I won't be your whore" (LH 75). David is unhappy with the marriage of Alcott and Cassandra.

Willie and Lester reach at the Chester Parker's home in the 'Fourth Crescent Drive', where the funeral would be done on 22nd December to his wife Lycentia Parker. He is the entertaining mourners the night before the funeral of his wife Lycentia. Lycentia was the leader of a group whose goal was to block a housing development in Putney Wayne in order to preserve values in Linden Hills and the group was supported by Nedeed for his development. This group symbolizes the two groups of sinners in Dante's Fourth Circle. The hoarders and the spendthrifts were forced to roll huge stones against one another. She often says to Parker,

"Chester, I'm going to do everything in my power to keep those dirty niggers out of our community." (LH 135)

She is not yet buried, but Parker has hired Willie and Lester to steam off the wall paper in her bedroom so that the room will be ready for Parker's next wife as soon as Lycentia is buried. When Willie hears a strange sound,

"Willie, eat it . . . Eat it. . . . (LH 145)

He dreams in his sleep and hears a sound of the cellar person Willa,

"Will he eat it? (LH 147)

He opens the glass door and runs down the dark corridor and he is shocked by seeing the ghostly figure, bloody snakes, and crumbling brown sweets that seem to stretch ahead of him into eternity. Willie could hear his heart beating again and again. Trembling, he reaches to gather the blankets and sheets tangled under his feet. It is too late to eat the stuff where Parker wrapped up for them. The cake... nothing like the cakes he had eaten at home. Willie's mind snaps around that last thought, it was nothing like the cakes he had ever eaten in anyone's home. But Nedeed said,

"It was no trouble, my wife baked it." (LH 146)

Willie doesn't believe the words of Luther, he thinks that there is always something different about food when it is straight out of someone's home, but the cake is too perfect and the way the butter, rum, and the raisins went down all smooth and easy, it doesn't give him much time to think about Luther's wife who is missing for the days together and nobody is cared about it. The novel says,

"---he had almost missed tasting her absence why would Nedeed lie?

(LH 147).

The next day mourners gather to hear the Reverend Michael T. Hollis's funeral service of Lycentia Parker. The Reverent lives at 000 Fifth Crescent Drive, This drive parallels Circle five in the Inferno, where the angry tear at each other and the melancholic bring forth a bubbly froth whenever they try to speak.

The same angry tear at each other, Hollis and Nedeed quarrel at Lycentia's funeral. Willie feels glad to meet Hollis because his house is very close to Luther's house. asks Hollis, "Do you ever see his wife?" he reacts indifferently and says why would I see any man's wife. Willie consoles him, after sometime Hollis freely explains about Luther, a bad example for the Linden Hills. Matthew Kaminski recognized that Naylor "...seems to be using the struggles of...Reverend Hollis to tell the reader that in the Afro-American community, success can be accompanied by a corruption of morals and the degradation of personal dreams." The author seems to suggest that it is better to live one's life according to his own wish.

As Lester and Willie have left Fifth Crescent Drive after funeral and enters Tupelo Drive. They pass through the first to fifth crescent drive which is parallel to the circle of Incontinence in Dante's Hell. Naylor has not included the circle of the Heretics in Linden Hills because her "sinners are at odds with themselves and not necessarily with God." (Ward 193).

Two twelve-foot brick pillars mark the entrance of Tupelo Drive is the last three levels of Linden Hills, where the most prestigious area of Linden Hills. This area matches the last three circles of Dante's Hell, the residence of willful sinners. Willa's physical and mental journey ends in the fire. Here author has given two choices to Willa. She can either die or she can surrender to her husband and suffer the same pain as previous wives of Nedeeds. She destroys the total generation of Luther Nedeed by coming out of the basement and holds Luther Nedeed with the child and jumps into the fire, Willa not only ends her life. She ends the dynasty of Luther Nedeed.

The novel does not bind itself to moving forward day by day at time or in Willie's and Willa's growing consciousness, but progresses by swift backward and self-assured leaps in time. Chronologically speaking, Laurel Dumont is already dead at the bottom of an empty swimming pool, but "the cry of an old woman calling a little girl home" (LH 216), the sound of the name "Laurel" in the air recalls the memory of Laurel Dumont as a child. There are other effects Naylor achieves by the smart organization of scenes in her novel. When Willie discovers Laurel at the bottom of the pool, "Without thinking, he turned her over" (LH 249). In italics the very next paragraph follows with, "Her face was gone." Naturally, the "her" in the italics does not refer to Laurel Dumont, but to Priscilla McGuire Nedeed who had simply erased her face with bleach in a photo album Willa came across. The continuity control is highly successful in imparting to the reader, who is abruptly wrenched out of one scene and thrown into another, the terrible physical reality of Laurel's suicide. "Perhaps the foremost effect of continuity editing is to efface the moment of transition between shots." (Pam Cook, 1990)

Naylor uses her creativity effect to intertwine her two parallel tales which are spatially separated although occurring simultaneously. Chapter 22nd December begins with Willie's nightmare and the chant of "Willie, eat it Eat it" (LH 145). Two pages later, Willa's tale is taken up again with the echo, "Will he eat it?" (LH 147). With her clever play on the sound of the words, Naylor makes the repetition echo in the reader's mind, again mysteriously connecting these two characters in spirit. Another example of Willie and Willa's parallel journeys can be found in the chapter 23rd December. By that time, their spiritual odysseys have fit together so far as to make it possible for them to have reached a common central and pivoting point in their thoughts. Willie lies in his bed composing a new poem in order to calm his troubled mind,

"There is a man in a house at the bottom of a hill. And his wife has no name" (LH 277).

Naylor develops on this creative technique by manufacturing a possible but once again improbable series of coincidences, timing the events of the novel so that they interlink neatly in the novel, pulling together to contain a complete story. The end of Linden Hills had caused critics discomfort, because far from delivering a blow at the patriarchal Lutheran tradition to delight the hearts of feminists, Willa simply desires to resume her life as a housewife and to do so in the Nedeed house, no less. Willa Prescott Nedeed does not desire revenge. This had amazed Naylor as much as it does the indignant feminist reader, and Naylor, with disarming charm, candidly admits as much,

"I said, 'Oh Lord, woman, don't you know what the end of this book has got to be? You've gotta tear that whole house down to the ground, or my book won't make any sense!' Obviously she didn't care. And I was angry with her for a good week - I just stopped writing and ran around the house cursing her." (The Southern Review 587)

Themes: Postcolonial Legacy

Once again Black woman becomes a victim of the Western materialism and Black patriarchy. Luther's conspiracy with colonial powers has empowered him to enslave his wife, his family, and his people. "Luther Nedeed, who functions as Naylor's 'worst case' scenario, a traitor to his family, his heritage, his community, and his 'ethnocentric sense of self'", is the Satan of Linden Hills (Christine 19). Luther Nedeed has not followed the pattern of his fathers, and he married a pale- skinned woman. He knows very well that those wives have been chosen for the colour of their spirits, not their faces. He actually has to pause a moment in order to remember his mother's first name, because everyone including his father has called her Mrs. Nedeed. The pale -skinned bride has given him a son, but a white son. The same squat bowlegs, the same protruding eyes and puffed lips. He looks at this whiteness and sees the destruction of five generations. The life of white son went unnamed and avoided by his father for the first five years and Luther tries to discover the reasons for the white Nedeed, through his wife. He takes out the journals and charts that are locked in his den.

He spent weeks in tracing the dates and times of conceptions, and the births for every Needed in Linden Hills. He then matches all of this with the position of the stars and the earth's axis. He concludes about his son, "There must be five days of conceptions at the appearance of Aries, and the son is born when the sun is died" (LH 19). So he likes to get the final opinion of the Doctor, after the medical check-up, nothing is abnormal with his reproductive organs. The medical report clearly states that,

"... there was no way that this child could be his son" (LH 19).

The pale - skinned wife became a constant irritant to him. The irritation began to fester in his mind and he wants to remove it. He can divorce her, but no one in his family had ever got divorced. Later she clearly understands that he has allowed her as a whore to Tupelo Drive only for child bearing not as a wife. Willa learns, "...a lot about the history of these socially highly respected Nedeed men.... Almost all the Nedeed women died in exile or in seclusion unseen and unheard by the neighbours."

Willa in the downstairs, an inability mother of the suffering child in the basement wants to save her son. Though she waits for the basement's doors to open with all her willfulness, she sees that she couldn't save her child. She would scream but decided not to. Every movement of the morgue wall clock's rusty gears make her mind swing with each "Sec- onds.... Sec-onds...." (LH 65). Luther cannot understand the wrong which took place. He has never been cruel or abusive her, never questioned what she bought or why. He taps his glass thoughtfully and goes near to the water valves under the kitchen sink and turn them on. Then he clicked on the intercom,

"Mrs. Nedeed, I'm giving you some water now. There will be no more food, Please catch as much as you can quickly because it won't be on all night" (LH 69).

She cannot bear the ticks of the clock. Painfully, she takes a deep breath and tries to go without the sound. But the spraying water from the valves forced different rhythms into her brain.

"Would this torture never end? Oh God, please stop that noise ---" (LH 70).

She doesn't move to collect the water because there is no longer any need of water, light, and food. She sits there calmly and irrevocably immersed in the simple fact that has become part of her being. Now she wants to lie down there and die on her own way. Her son is now in the cradle of her mind and to mourn she would have to remember. This alone will be enough to kill her. But the death of the child makes her to take revenge on Luther's generation. Then slowly she begins to smile and her lips started trembling from silent waves of laughter. Her laughter finally broke in hard, dry heaves as her fingers dig into her scalp. She bends farther over her knees coughs up phlegm and blood but she cannot stop, so she laughs and spit. She reaches up to wipe the tears away. Her breathing is still deep but evenly spaces as she wipes the mucus from her nose with her sweater sleeve. Indeed, it would kill her, but her mind reflects that,

"You're a coward even up to the end, aren't you?" (LH 91).

The wetness from the tears that cannot fall through her clenched eyes to smolder the burning fires in her head. She sits on the other cot and says, "I'm so sorry but I can't mourn you." It hurts her too much the way that her son died. She starts to wrap the body in the blanket it lay over but it is coarse and cheap, smelling of weeks of sickness and fever. She cannot leave as it is, so she goes to the corner and opens a trunk of old clothes. Her hand touches a gauzy film and she pulls out the end of a long bridal veil trimmed in yellowing lace. She keeps pulling the material and it seems to unravel forever so she digs into the trunk and extracts the folded veil. It is wrapped around a leather- and gold-bound Bible etched "LUWANA PACKERVILLE 1837" (LH 93). She turns the bible and tilts it towards the light, she reads, "There can be no God". She throws the Bible on the cot and begins to wrap the lace around the child's body but she hesitates before wrapping the face. She bends down and kisses the white forehead before she drapes the small face. She sits on the cot across from the shrouded body of her child with Luwana Packerville's Bible resting open, her eyes are watery from trying to interpret the fine. She could identify the oppressed life of Luwana Packerville, the wife of first Luther. She stares down the Bible in her lap. Trembling, she goes back to re-read the entry between the books of Genesis and Exodus. Her life had been buried in the book that Bible of her own; her letters and life placed between her wedding veil and Bible. Luwana had been a bondswoman to Luther as a wife. The author represents the experience of all the Nedeed wives with the help of Luwana,

"Luther told me today that I have no rights to my son. He owns the child as he owns me. I thought my sale to him was only a formality. I thought in the name of decency my husband would have destroyed the evidence of my cursed bondage. Foolish creature that I am, I have exchanged one master to another" (LH 117).

Willa comes to know about the two marriages of Luwana and gets confused about the past life of Luwana. Willa has now the key to Luwana Packerville's buried memories. Luwana's papers reveal the howling of a mistreated and isolated wife. Nedeed ignores her completely, once she has delivered the male heir he requires for next generation.

Evelyn had maintained very close relationship with cookbooks and recipes. She understands the sexual inadequacies of Nedeed, so she tried ancient method of cooking by using herbs to get the attention of her husband. The ingredients that Evelyn Creton hoped would make the crucial difference. First she cooks heavy meals in order to attract her husband's love, after that she followed old method of cooking, but was in futile. When she fails, her sexual aggravation and failure are expressed to be crazy with cooking and eating massive quantities of food, laxative, and prussic acid along with vanilla ice cream. She had documented a purchase of prussic acid with vanilla ice cream on December 24 which gives the clear sketch of her death. In anger, Willa tears up the cookbooks and scatters them over the room, she has been staring at Evelyn's last page for hour and unaware of the time and days spent in the cellar.

Willa unknowingly learns more about herself while learning about other faded lives of the wives of Luther Nedeed. Willa recollects her family background and her past life, a thirty-seven-year-old woman well educated from a reputed college and six years ago Willa Prescott married Luther Nedeed, became Willa Nedeed, and Willa Nedeed in a pair of suede boots walked into a place called Linden Hills. She married Luther Nedeed on her own choice because she wanted to be a Nedeed.

After all, every literate person in the Western world knows that the name Luther is a good name. She becomes a wife and less than a year later she gives birth to a son. Willa Nedeed has been a good mother and a good wife. For six years, she can claim that identity without any reservations. But now Willa Nedeed sits on a cot in a basement, no longer anyone's mother or anyone's wife. "So how did this happen?" (LH 279) a question still stays in her mind. Willa evaluated herself and thought that she is responsible for her life. She is caught down in the basement because of herself. When Luther had led her to the basement steps, she had walked down herself. She can walk back up whenever she is ready. The Bible, Cookbooks and Photographs have helped her to gain the power of revolt for the male tyrants.

Meantime, Willa meticulously folds and packs away the torn books and clothes. Importantly she fills the trunk with the pages from cookbooks, diaries and Pricilla's album on the top of the box. At last she goes to her child and lifts him up. She is so sorry for what she has done. The child had a chance to live. The child was just learning to write his name, so she had taught him to spell "Sinclair" (LH 294). Willa starts from basement to concrete steps when Luther is placing the final candles on the tree. On the other side Willa holds the child tightly and begins to climb the steps of the basement. There is no doubt about her path. It is coded into her being that twelve steps to the door, then into the kitchen. After cleaning that room, she would start on the den and then up the hall toward the staircase to the bedrooms. When she opens the door, Willie is shocked to see a woman, her hair tangled and matted, her sunken cheeks streaked with dirt. Her voice is cracked and husky as Willie's hand went toward his tightening throat,

"Luther" – your son is dead" (LH 299).

Luther spins around to the kitchen door. As the woman crosses the threshold, dragging the lace between her legs, Luther wants Willie and Lester to get out of the house to handle the situation. Both the friends are in bewildered face and trust their voices now. They stand there frozen for a long time, no way of telling exactly how long they stand.

Luther reaches for the child. The moment his fingers touch the wrapped body, making a fraction of space between it and Willa, her arms loosened for one to shoot around his neck, the other his waist and the three are welded together. Luther tries to wrench free, but they breathe as one, move as one, and one body lurch against the fireplace. The incident takes place in front of Lester and Willie. Lester suggests Willie not to call the cops, even he doesn't believe himself and no one will believe them. When they cross the lake of Tupelo Drive, they see smoke billowing from the side of the house as the den clothes go up in flames.

Willa had not been part of any community either before or after her marriage, a community in which she could find a shelter, and perhaps even a stronghold. She had not the opportunity of sharing in a sisterhood of women from whom she could draw the support and love withheld from her by her husband. When the lonely Willa accidentally discovers hand-written entries in an old Bible of a woman who lived many generations ago, this diary reignites her interest in living once again. Her own feeling "There can be no God" (LH 93), was written on the old Bible by another woman alerted Willa to the truth that someone in that house had perhaps suffered as she is suffering, to come to the same conclusion as herself. Exploring further, Willa takes the chance of bonding with a sisterhood of women among the women of the past, a sisterhood spanning across the ages to bring the same sharing and wisdom as belonging to a community would have done for Willa.

Willa begins to gain an understanding of facts in her own life. Watching the sufferings of Luwana, Willa as well as the reader is shown how a patriarchal order may sanction the psychological abuse and emotional starvation of women in a way that leaves no room for the women to understand the wrongs done to them. Willa sees that she herself was a slave to her fear of society's condemnation, marrying to set herself free from the social stigma of being single. As Willa begins to reflect, finding her own plight being the same as Luwana's on one level, she identifies so closely with Luwana. Willa has begun to think of her own life. Because Luwana was courageous to see that marriage had not set her free, Willa is heartened enough to follow suit, admitting to herself that freeing herself from social stigma had only forced her into the trap of society. Luwana Packerville fought her miseries bravely and in an attempt to bring comfort to herself, began to write letters to herself. In her letters, it is clear to see that there was a struggle to rationalise the action measured out to her by her husband, to certify if she had been wronged in any way.

Evelyn Creton who also married a Nedeed is not a woman who wrote diaries or letters to herself. Her legacy is left in recipe books and grocery records, another wholly feminine way of recording life and the trials of life. The third Mrs. Nedeed was an unsuspecting, happy, laughing, carefree Priscilla McGuire prior to her marriage. She had not been like the former Nedeed wives and Willa was cheered by the photographic evidence of her high spiritedness and happiness. She is a woman of individuality who managed to be unlike even within the restraints of agreement as it is witnessed in her photos. By this time, Willa had come so far in her understanding with the women who had occupied the same house as she did, shared in the same sufferings as she suffered, that she is able to predict the destruction of Priscilla when she sees that the lady is allowing herself to be shadowed by her son. Willa has learnt to see a pattern and be forewarned by it. There are few records of Priscilla apart from the photographs, but they are adequate to tell their story of self-mutilation the bleach on photos, the word "me" scrawled beneath the empty hole where her face should have been a course of action which is the same in essence as that of Luwana's or Evelyn's. Like the two before her, Priscilla sought to record her absence since no one else seemed to notice or care about it.

The Nedeed women are strong ones as they prove in their power of endurance and the terrific energy it must take to silence themselves and submit to their husbands. Their tragedy is that it was all misguided and misplaced energy, which destroys them instead of destroying their unhappiness. They are all wives who have been dehumanized by their husbands, women consumed with their silent, voiceless anger, silenced because they did not know they had a right to rage, and would not have known how to rage even if they had wished to. They are women who have been victimized without their knowledge and beyond their knowledge, losing their identities, their voices and then understanding in being Mrs. Nedeeds. They had unfortunately all give way to the natural female intuition of turning upon themselves when they found that by the standards of society, their husbands are apparently blameless. What they failed to question was the fairness of standards set by a patriarchal society. The Nedeed women had unknowingly committed the sin of self-treachery in their silence and ultimate acceptance of their husbands' ruling in their lives.

The records of the former Nedeed wives warn Willa of how things will be if she does not stop their worsening. Willa's initial response to this is anger, a healing, strength-giving anger, first misdirected at the dead women, then redirected at the wrongs in her life. As Lorde had identified in one of her presentations, anger can be put to good use, "Every woman has a well-stocked arsenal of anger potentially useful against those dominations, personal and institutional anger expressed and translated into action in the service of our vision and our future is a liberating and strengthening act" (Audre Lorde, 1984) Taking a step which had eluded the other Nedeed wives, Willa was able to make use of her anger in a healing process, then resolve that anger and put it aside, proceeding from there to a mental rebuilding of her life.

Laurel initially tries to resist such male humiliations but ultimately comes under the pressure of overpowering atmosphere she commits suicide by diving off the high board into an empty pool. By choosing death in place of tolerating male chauvinism, Laurel Dumont amply exhibited her confrontation under the circumstances. In fact, there are varieties of women or men characters in the novel, who bear violence and exile in the same way. One such character is Grandmother Tilson, who is also the prey of violence and exile. She bravely confronts Luther Nedeed. Although she is no more alive yet she had fought Luther Nedeed as the lone-fighter against his upward-striving black community. She had provided the catfish heads that Luther Nedeed used to make the female corpses seem alive as if passing on some principle of female vitality. But her all efforts go in vain when she finds negative response from middle-class residents. She resists the mal-tactics of Luther Nedeed and confronts him at herself giving her rebirth of strength and power.

Symbolism: An Allegorical Narrative

In an allegory reading, symbols addresses suggest sins of the characters. First Crescent Drive is Dante's first circle of the unbaptized Lester Tilson, Second Crescent is the second circle of the lustful Winston Alcott, Third Crescent is the third circle of the Gluttonous Xavier Donnell, Fourth Crescent is the fourth circle of the misers and the wastrels Chester Parker, Fifth Crescent is the fifth circle of the delivering angel Rev. Michael Hollis. Tupelo Drive is a combination of the last three of Dante's circle – a place for suicides Laural Dumont, hypocrites Daniel Braithwaite, and traitors Luther Nedeed.

The outside world perceives Linden Hills as a symbol of black achievement and is, "...precariously kept in place by the machinations of a wealthy black patriarchal family". The residents of Linden Hills know that Luther can make any changes on his house, building extra rooms and a third level. The people are heading for him, he succeeds because they bring their sweat back to his land and his hands and they believe that heaven is still waiting to be in new dimension "...a beautiful, black wad of spit right in the white eye of America" (LH 9). Luther's grandfather's dream is to make the Linden Hills a showcase... into a jewel --- an ebony jewel" (LH 9) that would mirror the soul of Wayne County as well as the pride of his people.

Just as in *Their Eyes Were Watching God*, Jody Stark refuses to eat Janie's cooked food apprehending poison in it, Luwana is also denied to cook for her husband and son, once when Nedeed comes to know of a slave who kills his owner by poising his soup.

Even she is refused to communicate with her son, only the habit of writing letters results in awakening her consciousness. When the law decrees that a child must follow the condition of its mother bondage, Luther one decides to celebrate manumission for his son by visiting the solicitor to draw up free papers for his son. The exact 665 times which Luwana's needed to open her mouth to speak – 332 times to answer their good morning's and 333 times to do the same in the evening. The author sensitively has made the mark on the body of Luther's bonded heroine. Luwana used the silver hat pin to carve a line on her chest and stomach, which then she rubs with ink until the bleeding stops, for each time she calls upon to speak throughout the year. And she carefully counts them all just before she sat down to write. There is no record of the happenings to Luwana Packerville in the morning, she made her six hundred and sixty- sixth utterance. Willa goes back to Luwana's last words ---

"Just that I fall on my knees and thank God in heaven for sending me you." But it couldn't end there, and it hadn't. She had found the end in the beginning: "There can be no God" (LH 125).

She puts down the Bible, goes over to touch the edges of the lace covering her son's body, and she starts crying. The last words of Luwana reveal the religious literate Afro-American women's slavery in the same Black society. Willa is on her knees, surrounded by piles of dusty, yellowing cookbooks. She has hoped to find some other records left by Luwana, but the woman seems to have disappeared. She opens the third card box and finds another stack of wire-bound recipes. She finds another ancestor, Evelyn Creton Nedeed and there is no need to open the covers and see that name written in large block letters on the inside. But she still digs into the box, hoping that something of Luwana may wedges in heavy cookbooks. Her heart quickens when she sees a wad of papers but finds only the columns of canning dates,

"Thirty quarts of snap beans, May 1892.

Twelve quarts of pickled tomatoes, September 1893.

Twenty pints of blackberry jam, August 1896" (LH 140).

Evelyn Creton has even documented the dates on which she has purchased and used the components for each recipe. Willa thinks her search is futile, but she still empties the box. At last she discovers two slim volumes covered in black silk. They are also recipe books, but the content confuses her, most of the ingredients are measured in ounces and pinches, and the dates are crammed together,

June 14th – Add: 2 pinches powdered dove's heard

6 amaranth seeds

1 pinch snakeroot (LH 147).

Naylor has said that the treatment of the Nedeed women symbolizes the way that men have regarded women throughout history, as means of generation that have no value in themselves. As far as men are concerned, women have no history because they do not really exist. Naylor through Willa's character not only shows the crucial life of a black woman but also tries to show the suffering, male dominance and the black male chauvinism. At the same time, she tries to raise her females to resist and revolt against male torment and gives them inspiration for re-shaping their life.

Two days are remaining for Christmas Eve, Luther thinks why he is alone? There is something so terribly wrong about people being alone on Christmas Eve. He will not have his family ending up like the Dumonts who are totally lost to Linden Hills. His own thought depresses him. Luther decides to bring his wife out of the basement on Christmas Eve. He has to start again because,

"If his own wife died, can he start again? there must always be Luther Nedeeds. There must be Christmas and Celebration. There Must be ..." (LH 288).

Luther gets up from his chair and headed for the kitchen. He turns the valves on under the sink full force before pressing the intercom,

"It's Christmas Eve, Mrs. Nedeed" (LH 288).

He moans through intercom. On Christmas Eve, Willie and Lester come to Luther's house to decorate the Christmas tree. Luther invites them, "Gentlemen, come in" (LH 289). As they step over the threshold and Luther closes the door against the freezing wind. They start to decorate the Christmas tree. Luther says Willie to place candles on the Christmas tree because there have always been candles on their trees, he couldn't imagine Christmas without candles on tree though candles are harmful. Luther begins to tell them as they fill up the rest of the tree.

"Did you know, gentlemen, that there's a story behind each of these? My great-great- grandfather lived in just such a ..." (LH 294)

However cleverly Luther Nedeed had manipulated others, whatever the depth of his understanding of human nature with its ambitions, blindnesses and desperations, Luther had never fully understood women. For Luther, providing his wife with money and material comforts justified his demand that she repays his generous input into her with obedience and a son the image of himself.

"....he could not understand what had gone wrong. He had never been cruel or abusive to her. He must have given her at least six lines of credit in his name and he asked so little of her in return simply honour what his family had done, just as he honoured it" (LH 68).

There is a language Willie and Lester communicate in, which Mrs. Tilson doesn't like it. Mrs. Tilson wishes her son to speak in the formal, standard, connect English of the majority of the Linden Hills residents, a form of English which signals good education, civilized manners and higher status in society. Luther Nedeed who is at the top of the social ladder and therefore at the geographical bottom of Linden Hills takes it one step further and speaks even more formally. The firm formality and rigidity of Luther Nedeed's language reflects his inflexibility of character and purpose. There is another type of language in the novel, which is the language of women. It is a wholly feminine language which may not communicate wholly by the expected rules of logic and rationale. It is a language Willa has to learn to read before she can find herself and her voice. This is a feminine language unheard by men and buried under time and silence. This is a language which requires understanding because it has lain forgotten and unappreciated for years, the language of all the past Mrs. Luther Nedeeds.

Conclusion

The ancestors of both the boys have faced violence as well as exile and, so both are grown up in gloomy atmosphere. Though they are free from slavery but somewhere they are in pressure by Luther Nedeed. When Luther's wife emerges out of basement, Willie and Lester were present in the Luther's house. Willa grips Luther and along with her dead son, jumps over the Christmas tree in front of the shocking eyes of both the boys. Although Willie and Lester were prepared to complain against Luther Nedeed's ill behavior in the society yet seeing the brutal end of his life they consider it an end of an evil person. Thus, one can find that each and every character of the novel face and bear the torment, humiliation and exile in the society either in one form or the other but every character at the end, resists such evil tactics and makes rebirth of their lost identity and dignity.

Braithwaite, the historian of Linden Hills, would have sold his soul for the key to this language had he known it existed. He had boasted that his is "the whole story, the real story" (LH 263), and had not realized that a essential part of the story lay in a bible, recipe books and a photo album. Braithwaite claimed to have had a "whole series of checks and balances from numerous sources" (LH 263), never knowing that his historical account of Linden Hills and the Nedeeds is necessarily an uneven description in the story because it lacks the records of the Mrs. Nedeeds.

CHAPTER FIVE

Mama Day: Exploring the Spirituality

"Time is a funny thing. I was always puzzled with the way a single day could stretch itself out to the point of eternity in your mind, all while years melted down into the fraction of a second."

--- Gloria Naylor, *Mama Day*

Introduction

Gloria Naylor wrote the novel *Mama Day* in 1988 with the hope to expose that one can overcome their pain and live a life accepting it as it comes. *Mama Day* was Naylor's first unchaptered novel. In *Mama Day*, she has combined her favorite characters and personality, creating George, the ultimate man and lover. Miranda Day is the wisest of conjure women, Cocoa, playful but shrewd modern black woman who take the overall strength of the "ancient mother of pure black that one day spits out this kindagol" (MD 48). It is not possible to explain Naylor's *Mama Day* in one way. *Mama Day* gives the enjoyment of both the classical novel which structured plot stuffed with replications and foreshadowing's and the folk tale with its oral tempo and mystical actions. The secret power of Naylor's patchwork quilt *Mama Day* brings the unreal characters face to face with human beings living through the pain, complexity and mystery of factual life.

Artistic Characters of the Novel

The central characters in the novel are Ophelia, Abigail and Miranda (Mama Day) who undergo hardships in their lives and are able to overcome it by their experience. Each character is linked with their personal imagery and language. They communicate in their own dialect. Houston A. Baker in his *Workings of the Spirit: The Poetics of Afro-American Women's writing* (1991) identifies "the power of conjuring to provide guidelines, control motivation and remedies for a black vernacular community grown out of the ancient, authentic African origins of its practices." *Mama Day* is written with the language of the southern, Willow Springs. George's mind is restricted, his terms are the accurate words of an educated city man. As part of Cocoa's role as walking the middle road, she thinks in city language, but often the Willow Springs dialect comes back, particularly when she is at her home.

Naylor uses three sporadic voices in the introductory pages. The first voice belongs to the knowledgeable Mama Day and her sister Abigail, the second voice belongs to Abigail's grand-daughter, a light brown skinned Ophelia, who lives in New York City and comes back to Willow Springs on the time of Candle Walk. This carnival is celebrated on 22nd December of every year. It is habitually celebrated after the harvesting of crops, which the natives cultivate in their fields. For the poor natives, the winter could be very hard due to lack of food and clothes. Candle Walk carnival is a mode of helping the poor without feeling obliged. People offer all sorts of stuff to each other without considering its financial value. In New York Cocoa meets George Andrews, who is an engineer, almost orphan and who gives the third voice for the story.

On the other hand, Miranda recalls her father and great grandfather, Boscombe, who was a Norwegian and got married to Sapphira, who was African-born and then came beneath the influence of slavery. With a bitter past of having only been permitted to the waste of the American society, it has become a topic of delight with African Americans that which others have deemed hopeless and unnecessary is rescued and distorted into articles of beauty and worth. Artistic design has passed into African American literary custom as a sign of the creativity and resilience of a race, a proof to the African American art of creativeness, change and endurance.

Naylor's expressive language exerts itself in other ways besides character development. The stormy shore of the Sound (an ocean) comes vibrantly to life, as does the mystery and majesty of the woodland. Cocoa has begun to dream from the poison Ruby has given her, and suffers through some dreadful pain. The awful imagery, the weal in her skin that began to move inside her body, the worms in the shower, the rot that takes a grasp of her insides, all affects the readers to a great extent and this is Naylor's greatest strength. Her words invoke emotions and deep distress for her characters is really the mark of a great author and an incredible novel.

Gloria Naylor steps away and allows the characters do her own work. Love has the fateful personality of being objective. She starts with Cocoa telling her side of things along with the character of George. This is a sparkling manipulation of point of views and one of the sustaining appearances of the book. The reader's interest is caught when they have to re-connect themselves to a latest point of vision. In the final representation of what love is this point of view proving similarity of thought between Ophelia and George toward the last part of the novel.

On the other hand, where Prospero revels in his skill to change the natural world with his magic, *Mama Day* accepts the boundaries of her power. *Mama Day's* character further departs from Prospero's fatherly egocentrism by her importance on female bonds.

Where The Tempest revolved around the envy and revengeful natures of Shakespeare's male characters, Mama Day is determined by the interconnections of the novel's women.

In *The Tempest*, Prospero needs revenge on his dishonest brother Antonio. In *Mama Day*, the novel arranges the characters' retracing of their female heritages. *Mama Day* tries to identify with the importance of three women in her life: Sapphira Wade, the slave who began the Day family line; Ophelia, Mama Day's mother; and Cocoa, Mama Day's grandniece (Erickson 244).

Mama Day is placed in difference to George Andrews, one representing the shrewd, cultured and knowledgeable, the other a properly educated, clever, logical man. Willow Springs, the area of a powerful female leader, Sapphira Wade, is spiritual, self-reliant, smooth and eternal. In the other world, New York symbolizes the victory of industrialization and knowledge, with all its energy, rapid transform and scientific discoveries of mankind. Naylor's characters are connected with each other and through this connectivity they represent the situation of female harmony. Strong society feeling is evident in the behavior of Miranda and Abigail, and it spreads through the whole island. Ruby filched the husband of another woman to persuade her sexual desire. Cocoa, on the other hand, also displays a character of black woman, who uses her husband, George at her will and wish. So, the novel is a reflection of black community and clearly reflects the women dominance and their bonding through their co-operation and active involvement in the society.

Female power and intelligence are vibrantly incarnated in the title character, Miranda alias Mama Day. She is not simply a mother to Ophelia, but a 'Grand Mother' to the entire community of Willow Springs,

"Mama Day says no, everybody says no" (MD 23).

She is a powerful conjure woman with unique gifts derived, in the community's view, from being a direct descendant of Sapphira Wade. She is an omnipotent woman and, so she makes Bernice fertile and calls down lightning to punish the murderous Ruby. Miranda has an unparalleled woman power, so she creates such an atmosphere, which is profitable for her well-wishers and against her opponents, "The men in the novel tend generously to support the women up to a point and are respected by Miranda for up-rightness and strength" (MD 24).

In the isolated island Willow Springs, Miranda works from side to side nature, as a midwife, as a death-dealer and as a daughter of the Mother deity. She redefines the group of gender conventions and rejoins the human society.

In *Mama Day*, two people who would apparently never end up together someway find a way to shape a relationship that finally leads to a marriage. George and Cocoa, the two lovers come from backgrounds that could not be different the other. George is a man who comes from the various and firmly administered city atmosphere of New York whereas Ophelia is a woman who was raised on the island of Willow Springs which is occupied by descendants of slaves and is subject to discrimination and disrespect for normal conduct in society. New York is a place where science and facts manage the decisions of days but Willow Springs has many customs based on magic and superstition. As the two sites are extremely opposite, it is hard for George to trust in anything that Cocoa was raised on. However, in order for George to get Mama Day's consent, he considers and appreciates magic as it exists in Willow Springs both in the form material and faith Gloria Naylor makes Mama Day the perfect conjuring woman character in this novel. She is very closer to her heredity than the rest of Willow Springs, as it is confirmed with her interactions with her late father and her knowledge while weaving the wedding quilt. Mama Day gets her power from her great grandmother. Mama Day goes after her foot path as a mid wife and herbal physician to her people. Apparently, the entire community called her Mama Day or Little Mama, even by her sister, she holds the honorary name of Mother.

Plot: The Human Relationships

Willow spring is a place on an island off the coast of South Carolina and Georgia that is colonized by the descendants of a slave population. There are several perspectives that a reader can take in explaining a variety of events that occur throughout the book.

In *Mama Day*, the verbal structure of the text is the most important tool that guarantees the readers involvement in the creation of sense. The beginning of the novel starts with a mythological island, which does not exist on any atlas but has a prosperous history and has a touch of mysteries. The author leaves the readers with the chance to answer them based on their individual experiences and beliefs. The collection of perspectives in

Gloria Naylor's *Mama Day* is personified in the legend of Sapphira Wade and the interaction betweenlogic and the supernatural and between George and Cocoa.

In this novel, Naylor combines her Southern background with her Northern location, expressing her warm regard of the African American woman and her bias towards the African American man, blending the supernatural and myth with colorless sensibility. There is much in Mama Day which rests on the edge of faith and this is what imparts a peculiarly African aroma to a story set in America. The whole story of *Mama Day* is apt to tell multiple love stories in it. Naylor doesn't tell a love story, but slightly lays out in detail the dealings of daily life for all of the central characters. In the process the love stories of the characters are all told at once. The best example is the relationship between George and Cocoa, the main love story. They meet, fall in love, and go through enthusiasm and adversity that the love affair of various people is framed in this novel. There is another love story of Mama Day, Abigail, and Cocoa. Even though Abigail is Cocoa's grandmother and Mama Day is her great-aunt, they both take on the responsibility of mother through their shared love for her. There is also the love story between Bernice, Ambush and Little Caesar. Despite their disputes, they love each other. Love is one of the main themes in this book.

Mama Day is a modern love story, a never-ending generational story, an amazing tale of the supernatural power and honor to the rescue power of African-American society. It is a book that spans into worlds. One is the southern barricade in island of Willow Springs, a place which is free not only from the rules of nature but from the cultural laws of men. God created the Universe in six days. Gloria Naylor has created her own universe in *Mama Day*. The other world, New York City has several different cultural and ruled by stern and apparently heartless rules of love. Naylor gives each of these worlds its own story and storyteller and then she fetches them together. With this prosperity of matter at her clearance, it is small wonder that Naylor's novels add a large component of intertextuality. Intertextuality is a quite modern growth in African

American literature, a present-day literary tool broadly used in Naylor's period of writing.

Naylor's reappraisal of Shakespeare's *The Tempest* in *Mama Day* not only embraces more women, but empowers them. Naylor creates a female, African-American edition of Prospero and leaves from *The Tempest's* importance on male supporting structures to stress the importance of female bonds. Like Shakespeare's romance, *Mama Day* takes place on a charmed, isolated island. However, Naylor refuses the imaginative offense in *The Tempest*. Naylor verifies the inhabitants argue to rights of their island like Caliban's pleadings in the tempest that "This Island's mine." Naylor's black islanders are strictly advised to guard their island from developers who would "...reduce them [the islanders] to Caliban-like servility" (Erickson 243).

In naming her determined protagonist Miranda, Naylor modifies Shakespeare's *The Tempest*. Naylor gives Miranda a second name as Mama Day further differing fromShakespeare's description. The name Mama Day suggests the original strength of Naylor's protagonist. According to Erickson, the age and experience of Naylor's Miranda not only contrasts with the youth and innocence of Shakespeare's Miranda but also Mama Day's scope also encompasses and outdoes Prospero himself. In dissimilarity to Shakespeare's Prospero, Naylor makes Mama Day not only more commanding and ethical, but also shifts the importance of the novel to the meaning of maintaining motherly bonds in African-American life. In *Mama Day*, Naylor struggle hard not to separate the non-African-American, but rather wish to widen the western cannon for the readers. Naylor, in representing the struggles of African-Americans, represents the important similarities between the African-American and non-African-American experience. Thus, Naylor universalizes literature to all surface of American society.

The sisterly bond is shown as thickened from a shadowy past and also accessible of the present relationship in the two sisters. But the plot of the novel is centered in the way which this bond is to be passed on to the hope, to Ophelia. Like her cousin Willa Nedeed, Ophelia is the success or of a female tradition. Whereas Willa's predecessor has all been isolated fatalities of men, Ophelia's ancestors has raised above men. Though they had also suffered, they have achieved a power that could be passed on directly. Although Ophelia has been raised in Willow Springs by Mama Day and Abigail, she is not fully alert of her fore mother's tradition or the evil represented by New York or by Ruby's distrust. She declines the voices at the churchyard and fails to know the message of her dreams, and she taunts at Mama Day's power together the New York job. The knowledge and power of sisterhood are yet to be fully conveyed to her and accepted by her. She has spent her ages nervously pursuing a livelihood in New York, but she still draws on the connection with Miranda and Abigail and her people by returning to Willow Springs. Thus, *Mama Day* falls into the tradition of other novels by black women in which strong women at the offset of the world help to identify the southern colored awareness largely through their associations with each other and their responsibility of culture.

The word feminism is a philosophy of women freedom as it is assumed that women suffer inequality because of their gender. And feminist is a woman who identifies herself, and is accepted by others as feminist. These type of alertness depends on a women having experienced consciousness rising, a knowledge of woman's domination and their difficulties and variance. In this novel, Naylor narrates the story of two black natives from noticeably different back grounds. An orphan from the urban North, George, has grown up in a foundation run by whites, and Cocoa, brought by two black mothers, soaked in the customs of the rural south. relationship develops between these two characters, one the product of the white world the other of an ardently black one, Gloria Naylor deals with the matter of preserving black cultural uniqueness in the face of attempts by the white world to organize, control and define black people.

Unspoken communication is essential in Willow Springs. The island belongs to the black people who live on it, since given the deed in 1823 by Bascombe Wade, a Norwegian. So the island, if it belonged to anyone other than the freed slaves belonged to Norway.

The black slaves of the island were tortured. They were not allowed to work on the field though they have paid all the taxes and revenues. They had to struggle throughout the lives whereas the white are to be the owners of the area because of their authority due to the white skin that they obsessed by birth.

The blacks were made to do only basic jobs. They had to face the cruelties, invective and rebukes on no reason. The error done was having a dark color. Besides, the women were not yet regard due revere or right. They too were kept in the same place as the men, as well the physical assaults they faced the racial dominations and sexual abuse. They were the second hand used items which were for minor jobs used for fun. The women of the Willow Spring are not left unaffected by sexual abuse. From the past generations, the women gave birth to many children. Woman spent her life in conceiving and delivering. The rest of the time was spent in taking care and looking after the children. So there was not much time left for her to spend on herself.

Naylor brings frontward the various stages the women that they undergo in justice throughout their life, their struggles, clashes and opposes the differences they come across in their life. These oppressions cannot be visualized but can be felt, they do not need words or actions but manners and mind-set too can cause the same despair. The women enter the chamber of agony in a natural way. Their action appears very common and natural but mistakenly they descend into the crushing hands of male soil take up many emotional decisions to control their sense of a wife mother and of a weaker sex.

Thus in the novel *Mama Day* feminism is marked not as presented conventionally by the black women writers. There is much of emotional cruelty by the male through words and behavior. But, a woman is shown very powerful, self-governing and with self identity, still has to face abuse, rebukes and tortures from the male members of the society in *Linden Hills* and *The women of Brewster Place*. The dark color has its vast blow at the mind ofthe women living at Willow Springs. Gloria Naylor makes it very apparent that the white is the dominating color. Beauty, qualities, attractiveness are only possessed under the white pigment ones. "It was torture competing with girls like that" (MD 233).

Gloria Naylor presents the sexual fault of man, their greed for sexual desire and displeased sexual desire that makes them worry wildly. They forget their status and position. They reveal their lack of control over their sense. They claim to be powerful and strong to the women but are unlucky to overcome the sexual needs. It weakens them secretly till they surrender. It continues till the end and the woman has to fight, defeat and get over this inequality on her at all levels of life. The major problem in this novel is the terms with one's own inheritance. Cocoa, resembles her great aunt Mama Day, has to understand her ancestral tradition and the spirit of Sapphira Wade, the originator of Willow Springs and fore mother. She comes to Willow Springs and inherits in the carnival Candle Walk, where people take to the road, candles in hand, welcoming one another with a line from a spiritual lead on carrying the light and exchanging gifts. Naylor has cleverly brought out the islands in the final battle. At last everyone believes Mama Day's supernatural powers as a subject of truth and is irritated with George for his powerlessness to do the same. Cocoa's life is dying out but saved through the combined sacrifice of her true well wishers. Her grandmother Abigail, Mama Day and George skepticism have overcome by the frightening sickness induced by Ruby's spell.

Naylor's *Mama Day* outstandingly resembles William Shakespeare's *The Tempest*, in both character work and design. The setting of each work is a strange isle paradise in which the islanders are directed by powerful magical leaders. The succession of the plot and character in *The Tempest* and in *Mama Day* act to highlight the supremacy and capabilities of black women. The reconsideration of power demonstrates Naylor's efforts to reconstruct the gender and cultural label present in Shakespeare's work. Naylor's borrowings from William Shakespeare's *The Tempest* in *Mama Day* can be reviewed on two faces. At first, George's affection to King Lear is observe thoroughly, on the second, relations between Willow Springs and *The Tempest* are tested, this double approach is related with the novel's overall geographic progress from North to South since George's Lear is situated in the former while The Tempest's associations are with the latter. King Lear specifically offers the common for negotiating George is seductive of Cocoa. George's reasonably superficial attachment to Shakespeare comes nowhere close to his adoring commitment to football. In Cocoa's case, she totally dislikes football matches because she believes and feels that players smell each other's behinds during the football playing, even Naylor herself shares cocoa's conflict to George's love of football.

The novel's second Shakespearean thread is the relationship between *The Tempest* and Naylor's image of the Southern island of Willow Springs, engages livelier encounter with Shakespeare. *Mama Day* has its line in *The Tempest*. The title character is Miranda refers to Prospero's daughter in The Tempest and Willow Springs is an isolated island whereas, on Prospero's isle, magical and mysterious events come to pass. In *The Tempest*, one part of the story concerns a delighted Miranda (Mama Day) and her obtaining, exercise and desertion of magical powers. The other story line concerns a pair of lovers Cocoa and

George Andrews. Willow Springs is an incredible island, magnificently situated. On this unbelievable island, one can see different forms of life as slavery and race relations, lover's quarrels, family associations and outrages, professional competitions and jealousness.

Themes: The Emotional Motherhood

Miranda, being a Mama of whole people, takes care and protects them from disaster and hardship. Mama Day does some magic against Ruby and her house. All these activities of Mama Day show her motherhood and care for her people. She is fully responsible for every decision of her citizens, so being mother of her relatives as well as natives; she does not dare to fight with anyone, "For black women history is a bridge defined along motherliness" (MD 25).

Unfortunately, George goes his way, in rationalistic skepticism and relying on his own strength alone. Ophelia has repeated the female pattern of breaking a man's heart as her perception foretold. Thus the gender clash seems unsettled at the end, with only a clue from Miranda of how it might be determined. Only in Ophelia's "conversation" with the departed George's spirit fourteen years later it can be seen perfectly as an open interaction between them, as she discovers and admits his point of view.

Mama Day arrives at a more composite vision of sisterhood. Naylor has stirred gradually from merely naturalistic to the representative and fabulous modes as well, as she adds chronological depth to the appearance of the female bond. She has stimulated away from a restricted focus on females to an exploration of the relationship between sisterhood and the resolution of the male-female disagreement. She has moved from a sight of the power of sisterhood as a guard from domination to a celebration of sisterhood as empowered by women tradition, by nature, and by enduring spiritual forces and from the strictly narrow and careful chance of sisterhood, to a wealthier and more optimistic glimpse of its reality, as it is in a community of women like those in Alice Walker's *The Color Purple*. If such a society of women is true to her thoughts, possibly she will style with it in her next inspiring effort.

The chronological relationship runs from the legendry spirit who founded the society, Sapphira Wade, all the way through Miranda Day to Ophelia. They have connected the gap of ancestral conjuring with African ancestry and the spiritual setting of their forefathers. Mama Day is a conjure woman and the emotional mother of the island. Sapphira is the spiritual mother of the island, she is considered to be the lineage 'Great Grant Mother' to everyone on the island. She is a fearsome existence that reminds the people of slavery, wrecked hearts, and the awesome power of nature. Everybody knows but nobody talks about the legend of Sapphira

Wade. Sapphire is

"A true conjure woman; She could walk through a lightning storm without being touched; grab a bolt of lightning in the palm of her hand; use the heat of the lightning to start the kindling under her medicine pot: depending upon which of us takes a mind to her" (MD 3).

She "turned the moon into slave, the stars into swaddling cloth, and healed the wounds of every creature walking up on two or down on four" (MD 3). Since she has refused to accept the role of a slave and because of her awareness of nature and female sexuality, she was given the title "witch". As mother, midwife, matriarch, and typical mother, Sapphira symbolize mother lines. She was a slave sold to Bascombe Wade in 1819,

"She married Bascombe Wade, bore him seven sons in just a thousand days, to put a dagger through his kidney and escape the hangman's noose, laughing in a burst of flames 1823: persuaded Bascombe Wade in a thousand days to deed all his slaves every inch of land in Willow Springs, poisoned him for his trouble" (MD 3).

The beneficiaries of this conjuring is property-owning, independent African-Americans of Willow Springs, respect Sapphira as their origin mother and the other place as her holy space. When she gave the family name "Day" to her seven sons, she cast herself as a motherly creator, mother of all of the Day, an identity Miranda underlines by referring to Sapphira as "the Mother who began the Days" (MD 262). Levin k. Amy explains that, "Sapphira becomes a mythical figure to the inhabitants of Willow Springs because she had the power to break her lover's heart and to get her freedom, even though the difficulty of her position as a slave woman." When Sapphira liberated herself from her white partner and master, Bascombe Wade, in 1823, she initiated a custom of female power and religious practice, Candle Walk; the inhabitants of Willow Springs grant additional food and supplies to families did not do well that year. They march throughout the town carrying candles, singing and chanting,

"Lead on with light, Great Mother Lead on with light." (MD 111).

Mama Day's mother Ophelia, in addition to have Abigail and Mama Day gave birth to Peace, who fell into a well. After her dead daughter, she jumped into The Sound, an ocean. She died, in Mama Day's terms, to find peace. Of Ophelia's three children only Abigail and Mama Day are left. Mama Day has no kids and Abigail had three Grace, Hope, and Peace. The importance of these names becomes clear and all three of these daughters are dead. Abigail's Peace died yet younger than the first Ophelia's. Left by her husband Grace is unable to recover from the pain of her own misfortune. Then, Miranda becomes not only a mother to her grandniece Ophelia but a "Mama" to the whole island of Willow Springs. From the first she is not only the society's midwife but also its protector of custom and its main authority figure. Abrahams explains that, "Afro-American children are taught to imitate their mother's behavior" and it is stated many times in the beginning that "Mama Day say no, everybody say no" (MD6), which demonstrates the strength and importance of Mama Day's influence and the unconditional respect for her role in the community.

Mama Day perceives magic in the woods on the island. She observes trees and flowers fluttering and hears them speak softly. Willow Springs' woods contain herbs, roots, stems and leaves that can be used for medicine and also poison. There is an undisclosed part of the woodland, where the supernatural things occur. Performers and spirits lurk in these woods; the rational gives way to the irrational. Mama Day's healing powers arise from the world of nature, from the plants and chickens she converts to medicine, from the trees and birds of the wood. Miranda's interaction with ancestral voices appears genuine and generally occurs during her lonely walks in the forest or during her time in the grave, actions that reveal with some fact of African beliefs about the dead. She talks to the plants, animals, wind and her ancestors. Miranda's family graves are in the forest, and all are arranged in seven groups, "old graves, and a little ways off, seven older again. All circled by them live oaks and hanging moss, over a rise from the tip of The sound" (MD 10).

Trees were planted in a straight line on graves to guide the spirits on their way into the earth. Miranda's amazing ability to see and hear is not always cloaked in vagueness. Her life span friend with the woods is answerable for her remarkable knowledge since, when younger, the whole island was her playground in which she'd walk through in a dry winter without snapping a single twig, disappear into the shadow of a summer cottonwood, so comfortable is she in the woods that folk started believing John-Paul's little girl became a spirit in the forest.

George explains Willow Springs as the paradise in Bible, "more than pure, it was primal" (MD 185). In spite of his admiration, George experiences a sense of objective and ideological displacement in Naylor's garden paradise. As he is not capable of recognizing the powers of women, the central conflict arises. Naylor intimates the single great basis of difference lies in an overturning, lasting ego of women power and its divine complement.

Though he observes the talented hands of Mama Day in helping the childless couple Bernice and Ambush and her magical powers of delivering the majority of the babies of Willow Springs, he discharges her powers and comments casually; natural remedies are truly at present. He calls Mama Day's medicinal tactic as "mumbo jumbo" (MD 295). The climactic action of Miranda's is,

"It (lightning) hits Ruby's twice and the second time the house explodes" (MD 273).

Miranda rationalizes her action against Ruby as an act of self-protection on behalf of the injured Cocoa. George senses this action as strange because a lightning strike twice in the same place is when "someone purposely electrifies the ground with materials that hold both negative and positive charges to increase the potential of having a target hit. No one was running around with that kind of knowledge in Willow Springs, and it was highly improbable that it would happen naturally." he ends (MD 274), but Mama Day undoubtedly did it. The exchange between Cocoa and her ancestors highlights the supernatural power in words, where words carry power to next generation. They cause good destiny, success, curse, peace, regret or blessings in moment of danger. When Ophelia is returned to life, Miranda feels that presently no secrets for Miranda herself to learn, that "the rest will lay in the hands of the Baby Girl --- once she learns how to listen" (MD 307). Thus, Cocoa becomes the next protector of the society of Willow Springs.

Mama Day, the story of the conjure women is a story of beginning Days. It is the story of the spirit of Africa that has toured to the New World on wood, wind and water. The conflict morals between the two standards of people generally results in the battle for the center of the protagonist. Using the tools of myths, ancestor-devotion, native mysticism, magic and the supernatural, Naylor's *Mama Day* redrafts the history of black community and specially the black women, who are able to change racism and chauvinism and the life with love in a country that works together to keep them fragmented and voiceless.

The Tempest, on the other hand, emphasizes remorse and forgiveness as a prologue to the re-establishment of an immediate order. *Mama Day*, emotional connections, empathy or kindness, respect for great natural powers and savage revenge against basic disloyalty of the social bond. Gloria Naylor's *Mama Day* greatly resembles Shakespeare's *The Tempest*. Naylor not only inspired with the black women's survival and struggle but also stirred with the Shakespearean dramas and everywhere uses the plays of Shakespeare in her novels as The Women of Brewster Place, in the character of Kiswana, her fiancé Ambush, generally reveals the shows of Shakespearean plays. Naylor is much impressed with the play *The Tempest* and brings out the same island in which Prospero made in *The Tempest*. Prospero was the King of that particular island and Miranda in *Mama Day* is the queen of the island 'Willow Springs, Naylor suits the Shakespearean play to craft the female conquered island of Willow Springs, which inversely mirrors the male dominated island of *The Tempest*. *The Tempest* and *Mama Day* split islands situation, sorceress or conjurer in Prospero and Miranda, great storms which isolate people on the island, serious usurpers in the false king of Naples and Ruby, a witch comic usurpers in Stephano and Dr. Buzzard representatives of suitors from the brave new world in Ferdinand and George. Mama Day's given name, Miranda was a Shakespearean exploration is seen original in *The Tempest*.

In addition, as Prospero uses his magic to meet his own daughter Miranda with her fiancé Ferdinand, exactly Mama Day makes such basis, in which George and Cocoa meet each other. Prospero through his magical power controls the people. And through her supernatural powers she controls and protects the Willow Springs and its people. As Prospero uses his magic to control Caliban with the crudest nature of corporeal punishment and finally liberates Ariel, exactly Mama Day uses her powers to control storm, Bernice and witch Ruby and sets free Junior Lee from Ruby's trap. Thus, control is essential to the use of magic-control of creatures, spirits, natural elements and lastly other beings. Finally, in order to leave the island and rejoin human society, Prospero has to leave the island. On the other hand, Miranda has a great and tremendous power but she, by contrast, does not exactly practice magic. She mostly uses her herbs as well as seeds and relies upon the arranged waiting period. Through this practice and behavior, she usually heals her patients, so her attraction consists of emotional approach helped by the useful signs, Unlike Prospero's magic, Miranda's work exists firmly within the natural context, and Thus, *Mama Day* really resembles William Shakespeare's *The Tempest*. Annotated Bibliography on Gloria Naylor shows, "The two stories incorporate community alcoholics, a twisted subplot to usurp the leadership, and a ravishing storm, or tempest." The inversion of plot and characters in *The Tempest* and *Mama Day* functions to highlight the power and capabilities of black women. Certainly, it can be concluded that Gloria Naylor has taken a prompt sign from the Shakespeare's The Tempest for creating her novel more inspiring and by this effort her novel becomes one of her best novels.

In Naylor's *Mama Day*, Miranda is an eternal fixture in family space, baking cakes from scratch and nurturing the garden. Her domesticity gently extends into her healing work; she depends on the products from the garden and in the woods for the remedies she acquires for the community. Her role as midwife and nurse are not separated from her domesticity. Miranda's gifted hands are indeed a gift passed down through the generations of the Day family. As a people healer and midwife, Miranda holds in her hands a unknown and persuade that the people of Willow Springs respect with fear because she has skills and knowledge that no one fully understands her. Furthermore, as a successor of the greatest conjure woman on ground, Sapphira Wade, Mama Day's magical power is unquestionable. *Mama Day* definitely demonstrates a great deal of power, both religious and spiritual, and it is clear that her opinion carries a great deal of sway among the people of Willow Springs. The island is often described as speaking to Mama Day, and the voice is often connected to the spiritual presence of the Sapphira Wade. Because Miranda is a direct descendent of Sapphira, she is able to connect the power of the island and of her incredible ancestor, and she is able to do unbelievable things because of this spiritual connection.

Mama Day is able to use her spiritual link with the past and with others to help the people in this life through these acts. The confirmation of life that Mama Day demonstrates in her actions is a result of a spiritual connection to the island and its inhabitants. Mama Day has come to receive joy from life, and to see life as so important that protecting and nurturing as it becomes her own life's intention.**Symbolism: The Ancestral Inheritance**

There are some delightful examples of the differences in culture and moral importance in the North-South comparisons which it would be a disgrace to bypass. One of the most remarkable differences in Willow Springs and the Western world is using the way of measurement. Time is not measured in seconds, minutes and hours, days and weeks to years. Time is not measured by seasons and in one's memory. While calculating the age of Ruby, Mama Day recalls, like an African narrator, spiritually and orally keeping the records of the past and ancestry of his people, so too does Mama Day serve her community. George is bewildered by the total lack of purpose, standard, separate forms of measuring policy when presented with the family grave, the sizes of the headstones represented the missing dates -but only in relationship to each other - (MD 218).

As the logical engineer from across the bridge, he asks for performance of sales, records and names. Mama Day works by touch, while George works by thinking. Mama Day would have found no use for the metric system which rules George's life as she determines skillfully in terms that,

"she gets herself a piece about long as half a hand" "and then cuts a piece about the size of the last joint on her little finger It could kill as easy as cure" (MD81 - 82).

This novel crafts a breach in an almost mystical kingdom where everyone old and young, male and female, can be heard. Willow Springs is a place beyond the link to everyday life and reality and not found on a map, listen to and deal with those beyond the kingdom of the living Miranda and Cocoa go to the people churchyard to share their lives and tribulations. In this novel people go unheard because they converse noiselessly or because they converse with no words.

Sisterhood in *Mama Day* also involves working out relationships between women and men. Ophelia dies and the chronological line of conjuring women will also die out unless she is saved by George. Only through his sacrificial death Ophelia recovers from Ruby's tricks and takes over the sisterly inheritance from the past. George's death also makes it happen for Miranda to die in peace closely when she plans at the beginning of the new century. Naylor shows that the women can go afar men and have power of their own, but often at the cost of the disastrous loss for men. The men in the novel kindly support the women up to a point and are respected by Miranda for ethics and power. Bascombe Wade had freed his slaves out of love for Sapphira, yet he didn't allow her to go, the possessiveness of male love. Bernice's Ambush and Ophelia's George offer their wives a rich love, but George is limited by childhood insecurities and firm manly behavior toward women miscommunication.

The principal power of magic on the island of Willow Springs is Mama Day. A successor of the famous Sapphira Wade, Mama Day is said to have convinced her master to give the land that is Willow Springs to the bonds, for which she bore him seven sons in less than a thousand days, to put a dagger through his kidney and escape the hangman noose, laughing in a burst of flames. The power of Sapphira's magic is carried over into Mama Day, as it is said that she could,

"...walk through a lighting storm without being touched; grab a bolt of lightning in her hand; use the heat of lightning to start the kindling going under the medicine pot" (MD 91).

For a balanced minded person like George, this and some of the other customs are hard to accept. One such instance of George's ideas of normal human actions clashing with Mama Day's occurs when Mama Day and Grandmother Abigail give the married couple a quilt made completely of articles of clothing from past generations. George's first impulse is to protect it. He realizes, however, that the thing was not meant to look, but to be worn. What Mama Day wants most is for George to make Willow Spring a part of him before he takes Cocoa, a part of Willow Springs. She feels that he wants to become more conscious of the way they live and accept and experience their way of life in order to understand Cocoa desire.

To do this, George becomes more complicated in the society and undergoes experiences which are very unusual to him. A major example of this is his reaction to the traditions of Willow Springs on observing a funeral of a child. The ceremony is concerned with the mother hauling her dead child to Mama Day's home when the child was evidently dead. His reaction tells his horror, "No, this was the stuff of dreams. I spoke because I needed to hear the reality of my personal voice, although my question was as insane as the answer I received: 'She's going to the other place" (MD 258).

The tremendous case of George's disappointment to accept magic occurs when Cocoa is sick. He cannot trust that the herbal conjure of Mama Day will cure her better than modern treatment, and shouts to Mama Day about this saying, It's cruel to play these games when it's your own niece who is sick." This appearance brings forth George's opinion on conjuring. He fully discards it and sees it as an entertainment and not reality. Cocoa's view of herbal treatment, however, is opposite to that of George's. She accepts the curative techniques from Mama Day and exclaims to George by saying, these were the women who raised me-

"I would trust them with my days and so everything Mama Day had done is was for a good reason. But you refused to share my optimism---" (MD 273).

She knows that Mama Day's treatment work, and that Mama Day cares about her and wouldn't use them if not they did. In a similar way George fails to believe the conjuring methods of Mama Day and Cocoa is not able to accept George for doing this.

Mama Day is a woman with supernatural powers and magic. Through her powers and magic, she helps and controls the Willow Springs. Ruby, a witch creates an artificial tempestuous ambiance, aiming Mama Day's dearest one Cocoa, Naylor shows Ruby's fascination as the foundation of disorder and evil within the community. Naylor has the ability to believe and writes with the power of knowing that, anything is possible. Miranda generally does not practice magic but when she feels that it is very important for the wellbeing of the people, she ultimately uses her magical power and strength. Some of Miranda's 'magic' consists of psychological approach helped by the useful symbol. Miranda knows the assorted powers of roots and having been trained in her sensitivities, through a long time can identify, hear or see beggar's portrayal in the well-known landscape. Therefore, she is the Goddess of the island, who suffers from some dreadful fault but in spite of it, for the goodness of Willow Springs, she loses George who is very close to her. It can safely be concluded that *Mama Day*, a symbol of motherhood acquires the power and magic, which make her sturdy and superior amid the people of Willow Springs. Her powers lie not just in herbal remedies or conjure spells but they originate from deep misery of the mind and perhaps from very old sources of supremacy.

Miranda day receives the name "Mama" not because she has many children of her own, she has no one but because as midwife, she has formed or delivered most of residents of Willow Springs. She has served as mother not only to her blood relatives but to the islanders, she has brought into the world, is accepted as the most commanding conjurist on the island.

Mama Day gives up her option to be a daughter because she must care for her own mother who weeps for a dead child, silence, and begs her husband,

"Let me go with Peace" into the well that claimed their child's life (MD 284).

Mama Day is enforced to raise her sister after her mother's suicide and she is a self-sacrificing character enforced into the role of family concierge. When she is a child; she gives up the option to be a mother because she must care for everyone else's children, she mourns the loss of her childhood because she had "No time to be young" (MD 88). For Mama Day, there were no arms to hold her up, no shoulders for her to lay her head down and cry on, no body to ever turn to for answers.

Conclusion

Gloria Naylor makes no undisclosed of her faith in the supernatural. "I happen to believe that there are some people who can take you, or even take their own minds, to other planes. I believe in psychics. Naylor makes it clear what her beliefs are, "I believe in the power of love and the power of magic--sometimes I think they are one and the same. Mama is about the fact that the real basic magic is the relating of the human prospective and that if we reach inside ourselves we can create miracles" (Fowler 92). Naylor's Mama Day is a novel full of conjure --- Ruby, Dr. Buzzard, the motherly ancestor Sapphire Wade -- - besides Miranda (Mama Day).

Miranda remembers her father efforts to convince her and realize the importance of her role by saying, "I can't hold this home together by myself. And Abby, she ain't strong like you. We need you, Little Mama" (MD 89). To be there for sister, child and Being there to grab so many babies that plunge into her hands. Everybody's mama now and because of her multiple roles as healer, midwife and community leader, develops conventional ideas of motherhood. She representatively serves as the 'provider of life' for the residents of the island. She is not only a black American conjurer but a magician and doctor too. Mama Day is not a natural mother, her situation as creator is recognized through her close relationship to the natural world. She is the leader of the women in Willow Springs. Mama Day orders have the power and respect. Her age adds to her charisma and to her image as intelligent woman and eternal mother. The voice of the island suggests that she "is about as close to eternity anybody can come" (MD 7). Miranda worries and cares about the inhabitants of Willow Springs and her definition of family is open enough to embrace the entire black Community. Miranda safeguards the entry of birth and fatality, bringing her curative powers of growth to the natural world. Once, she has learned earlier that

"there is more to be known behind what the eyes can see" (MD 36).

Conclusion

This chapter summarizes the findings of the proposed research work. This book is a detailed study in Naylor's great artistic sense of decorating her novels with literary devices. It was planned to pick examples of her artistic and writing skills from her novels. The novelist's artistry rests in the depiction of characters, themes, plot, language, figures of speech, and symbolism and this book is focused on these principles in Naylor's three selected novels: *The Women of Brewster Place, Linden Hills, and Mama Day*. A brief study on *Bailey cafe* and *The Men of Brewster Place* is also performed for the substantiality of this research. She is cherished in educational circles and is recognized in the realm of literary society. Naylor is precisely acknowledged for speaking out the rights of women and other collective issues.

Naylor belongs to the group of Afro-American writers who have contributed their literary skills in the development of the genre by exploring the concept of identity and female relationship, at the same time, she has created a concrete province for her characters to develop under the situation of lost and uninhibited lives. A thorough study of the life and writings of Gloria Naylor exposes that she is a noteworthy and unique African American woman writer of the twenty first century, who projects the Black people and their society with its magnificence and glory. The Norton Anthology of African American Literature labels her as one of the first Afro-American female writer, who has the knowledge of both the ancestry of Africans and traditions of Europe.

The struggle for freedom - social, emotional, and aesthetic - is the distinguishing attribution of African American fiction from its origins during slavery to its pluralistic flowering in the twentieth century. Although the impact of the struggle has only intermittently been simple or direct, it has its perpetuity remained a constant presence, both on writers concentrating on the continual oppression of the black community and those forging highly individualistic poetic voices and unconcerned towards racial issues.

African-American literature revolves around themes like effects of racism, religion, slavery, a sense of homelessness, segregation, migration, realism, naturalism, modernism, feminism and inequality in the African-Americans life which reflects in their interaction with individuals and the groups in the society. Major themes of African American poetry include demanding the abolition of racial discrimination, demanding social equality, freedom and democratic themes of privacy of vision, complexity of allusions, and syntactical denseness. The positive approach of Naylor on the negative characters and negative signs such as lesbianism, homosexualism, and male domination within the same society are finest element of her writing skills.

Naylor showed a perfect escalation of her writing skills with each consecutive novel, establishing herself as an influential writer who never knelt before the social inhibition. After a century, the first novel by an Afro - American woman bravely represents lesbianism in *The Women of Brewster Place* and in the second novel *Linden Hills*, she spoke about homosexuality and other notorious issues. As a powerful author, she is capable of making her points with designed consciousness to the level of understanding. She sketches the urban lifestyles of African American people and celebrate the human nature in all forms. In all her novels, she technically handles good and bad and triumph and fall. She not only handles serious and highly poignant matters with stability, but also with generous sensitivity. As a writer of 21st century, she has written extensive literature on African American people. She has brought out the inner vibrant affinity of the Black culture while writing against racism, religion, slavery, segregation, migration, feminism and inequality.

Naylor linked all stories together, her first story is linked with the second and the second with the third and so on. This is an example of her uniqueness. She normally uses this strategy to create a rational connection from the plot of one novel to the other. The best example can be taken from *Mama Day* which is her third novel. It gives the beginning of George on her fourth novel Bailey's Cafe. Gloria Naylor stands as a model to contemporary writers of fiction because she herself is a part of all writings. Her novels are often inspired by her appreciation of literary giants like William Shakespeare, Dante, Toni Morrison and from her personal life. For example: *Linden Hills* is a version of Dante's *Inferno* and in the similar way *Mama Day* has the influence of *The Tempest* by William Shakespeare in addition to it Toni Morrison's *Song of Solomon* has the same influence.

Gloria Naylor's narrative techniques are magnificent. In her first novel, *The Women of Brewster Place* Naylor portraits a new depiction of relationship among women, woman friendship, sisterhood, and communal harmony. The first half of the novel completely presents imaginable approaches for existence, like nursing and joint supportiveness. In the second part of the novel Naylor presents the gradually collapse of a composite community. Naylor, in this novel, gives the impression by highlighting the prominence of traditional values and communal relationship of African American, and penetrative study into human psychology through thorough analysis of the lives of African American women characters. She creates the realistic image of agony and pain which these women undergo not only by white masters but also within their own society.

Through the imaginary characters and places Naylor is fascinated in bringing up the fact that the Afro - American women can growth and shape themselves within their colored community itself. Figuratively, it is made obvious that the creativity of Naylor brings the coverlet imagery of the past, present, and future.

According to Naylor, colored women obtain massive power and mental strength for their development and growth, through their experience from the past. She strongly believes and creates the imagery in her novels that the emancipation of women can become a victory through an understanding of their origins.

Time and again, Naylor exhibits her writing skills by creating the number of 'seven' characters in her novels. The number seven appears again and again to play an important role in her artistic skill. In *The Women of Brewster Place* and *The Men of Brewster Place,* there are seven female and major male characters. In the second novel Linden Hills is created by Luther Nedeed in seven days and in the unchaptered and third novel Mama Day, Sapphira Wade relaxed on the seventh day after completing her master deed his land to her issues. In *Bailey's Cafe* she launches six major women characters and a male character disguises in woman clothing to complete the artistic number seven. The novel *The Women of Brewster Place* projecting the seven female characters won her hasty fame, so within five years the novel was subjected into a movie starring Oprah Winfrey. The number of 'seven' and seven characters play a powerful role, in the writing of Naylor's other work and she, again and again, uses this technique in her novel. Naylor's artistry introduced a new patterns and colors as she adds to the Afro- American Literary writings by her artistic skills. She deals with the problems of women's language, culture, materialism and identity, the relationship between black women and men of Afro- American society.

As an accomplished author Naylor is well aware of her characters. Naylor's writings are placed side by side especially with other associated texts, namely the writings of her predecessors and contemporaries. A number of intertextual basics can be identified in Naylor's writings. In 1960s, Julia Kristeva a French philosopher termed the word Intertextuality. Intertextuality is a quality credited to postmodern writings which means valuating the meaning of a text by another text.

Naylor's writings can be positioned in the postmodern style because she surveys the factual condition of mind of the characters in her novels which is a leading feature of postmodern writings. Most of the characters in her novels are concerned with psyche of people, the characters like Mattie, Ben, Willa, and Laurel experience a psychological disturbance. Naylor has beautifully sketched the emotional oppression of the people in her writings. Such basics serve to contextualize Naylor's work, and more, to highlight the literary words (intertextuality) within it, an intertextuality which heretofore had not been possibly given the narrow accessibility of literary works by Afro - American women writers before the 1970s. Some of the critics have found *The Men of Brewster Place* has intertextual basics from *The Women of Brewster Place* because both the novels sketch the same backdrop. Besides, except one all other major male characters in *The Men of Brewster Place* are from *The women of Brewster Place*. Willa from Linden Hills is the grandniece of Miranda Day in the novel *Mama Day*. The character George from *Mama Day* is the son of virgin mother Mariam, who is in *Bailey's café*.

Naylor's works have been discussed in this proposal. The prominent issues discussed are socio-economic defeat of women, women bonding, women's sexuality, the language of women, and the adjustment of female characters in her novels. Naylor is a part of the Afro - American literary custom, particularly as a women writer. Hence, it is obvious that Naylor's artistic skills reflects throughout her novels to exhibit the life of Afro- Americans.

In many novels written by African American writers there is a prominence of emotional dearth and lonesomeness in female protagonists. Naylor, in the first entire novel, embraced the contact and relationship of seven women who were thrown collectively in close juxtaposition to one another when they all settled on Brewster Place. Female bonding and emotional telepathy among the women are the example along which the seven chapters of *The Women of Brewster Place* are joined together. Brewster Place was first sprinkled with champagne, and with blood and vomit. The baptisms strongly represent the vast gap between the promised and the unconvinced American dream. Naylor's novel is about the women managing and living in a men's society, and in a white humanity. Distressed approval is the answer to Brewster Place's endurance, and celebrated by its author. Having been brought up by Southern parents in New York, Naylor has a deep high belief for the folk knowledge, customs and beauty of the South. She is not mainly a Southern writer like Alice Walker, but Naylor does bring the North and the South into gorgeous contrast to emphasize the African American traditions and its development.

These Afro-American authors have worked within the black custom to protest against racial discrimination, but Naylor had changed her point of view from this style and looked backward to the folk tradition as the resources of creativity, celebrating the inner strength and highlighting the cultural richness of the society which she believes to be preserved and celebrated. Naylor's contribution to the literary world of Afro- American Literature is the development of narrative technique. She radiantly portrays the different types of characters in her stories like attractive, charming and unbelievable. In her stories, she sketches the feelings of the people and analyses their issues in a very accomplished style. Naylor states in *Contemporary African American Novel (1999)*:

"I wanted to become a writer because I felt that my presence as a Black woman in general had been underrepresented in American Literature". (29)

Naylor's novels also normally contain portions of her personal life and the history of her family in the general form of names, places and also stories. Her novels are connected and associated with each other. She refers to places and characters in a story which continues to be significant in the next text. She also draws widely from the Bible which clearly reflects the influence of her connection with the Jehovah's Witnesses, which impersonates her ethical and spiritual sensibilities.

The aim behind the artwork of *Linden Hills* is mainly resistance and rebirth. Naylor has emphasized that an attempt to supersede the white dominant society through economic means results into a shallow victory. The first idea of this novel is rooted by her reading of Dante's *The Inferno* in a Great Literature course. *Linden Hills* is an African- American middle-class neighborhood elegant after the encircling geography of Dante's Hell. Two younger poets, outsiders in Linden Hills who are looking for employment the week prior to Christmas, find out the obsession and crime of the middle class residents, who have abandoned culture and standards for materialism. All the characters have been represented elaborately through the eyes of two young poets. Naylor vividly depicts the pain, individuality, class consciousness, suppressed feelings, the approaches and battles of her characters through simple actions. In this novel Naylor depicts the ancestry of Willa which is one of the evidence of her skills that everyone pursues the frequency of ancestors in our unconscious mind.

Mama Day is an extraordinary novel with colorful descriptions and interesting characters. Naylor weaves an artistic saga with the unbelievable events that she describes in her characters is believable and act like authentic inhabitants. Naylor's most excellent skill is her significant powers, which not merely sets the view of the story, but fascinates the readers into Cocoa's twin worlds of Willow Springs and New York City, attracting them with her words. The fantastic mélange of colors and smoothness caught up in the quilt, overcome the mind of the reader through the richness of Naylor's artistic words.

Naylor enhances the connection of Mama Day with nature by associating her with natural imagery. Angelita Reyes calls the art of Naylor as "technician of the unseen the spiritual world" (185). The best example of Naylor's artistic aim can be deciphered in *Mama Day*. It is a representation alarmed womanist matters, African American literaryand physical traditions, and an absolute attractiveness in the usage of the language. It is a method of expression and a visual representation of the mutual efforts of the women. It has been noted by many critics that the mixture of beauty and utility of artistic design perfectly reflects the creativity of African Americans, a creativity severely restricted by the weary, incessant reality and necessities of day-to-day living. Naylor showed the importance of the family connections with the ancestors so that the very old traditions, belief, and divine wisdom of grandmothers might be of great assistance to their daughters and granddaughters to recover their individuality and personality in the perspective of the American society.

Naylor deviates from other Afro-American writers in her narrative technique. In all her novels she has introduced the Dawn and Dusk i.e. prologue and epilogue. She constructs her novels in the sequence of minor plots that together compose a larger text, except her third and unchaptered novel Mama Day. Naylor's writing style includes a nominal complex sentence arrangement which is quite accessible to readers. Most of her novels found to be changing between narrative characters. In Mama Day, She devices interchanging narrators which both echoes and supports the thematic concerns with sanity and reality of the novel.

The novel is about inspecting, analyzing and redefining the history of Africans. It is the matured writing skill of Naylor, how she brings forth the creativity to the people that the fundamental mystic is unfolding the human potential and reaches oneself deeply and the one can make miracles. This novel explains the importance of the tradition that all characters are made to be inspirational in the path of Mama Day. It is clearly visualized that all the characters accept and surrender to Mama Day's opinion and the spiritual feeling is created by the depiction of medicinal plants. Naylor inherit the creativity of this novel from their ancestors and she has a strong belief in the superstitions.

About Naylor's way of writing, different writers have different range of vision that she presents a fresh picture of relationships among women, female friendship, sisterhood, and community. Naylor's rewriting of the sixteenth century works of English rebirth, particularly those of Shakespeare, in her first three novels. Naylor is a talented author at giving world literature an African-American spin. Her works undoubtedly craft the fact-*Mama Day* of Naylor lends a lot from *The Tempest* by William Shakespeare. In this novel, Naylor combines her Southern surroundings with her Northern environment, expressing her warm appreciation of the African American woman and her bias towards the African American man, blending magic and myth with ordinary realism. There is a lot in *Mama Day* which perches on the border of faith, and this is what imparts a noticeably Africanaroma to a tale placed in America.

Naylor's account of life style and manner of thinking and level of artistic style, approaches, practice and beliefs are the extended scope of her individual image and self-confidence. This impact is easily viewed by the readers in the novels of Naylor in which she speaks and to which she is one of it. Her creativity is written in the first person and the fictive description is conversed as perfect accuracy as if the entire artistry materializes from the personal experience. In an interview with Charles Rowell, Gloria Naylor states:

I've ever lived, or ever wanted to live as a black woman comes out in my work.......You came age implicitly being told it is the white male world ... Everything that has lasted, has been just that their buddies kept them in the canon. (369)

This book has several implications. First, the book has highlighted the significant aspects of the African American literature in terms of plot, themes, character and symbolism. The bookhas made a thorough analysis of these literary aspects in Gloria Naylor's novels and found that she used these literary devices very dexterously which speaks of her artistry skills in writing fiction and narrating the psychological state of her mind.

Artists and artistry have existed in every human culture throughout the world and throughout history, as our author Gloria Naylor in this research work. Art and fiction are important ways in which we communicate to each other our understanding of what the world is like and how we have experienced it. Works of Naylor create a clear picture of her people's world that all appreciate and understand, whether the artistry been made with the strokes of a paint brush on a canvas or with words on a page like the novels of Naylor. When we look at amazing pieces of art, we can be transported to imaginative worlds unfamiliar to us, but we can readily believe that these worlds exist.

Works Cited

Primary Sources

Naylor, Gloria. *The Women of Brewster Place* .New York: Penguin Books, 1982. Print.

---. *Linden Hills*. New York: Ticknor and Fields, 1985. Print.

---.*Mama Day*. New York: Vintage Contemporaries, 1988.Print.

---. *Bailey's Café*. New York: Vintage Books, 1992. Print.

---.*The Men of Brewster Place*. New York: Hyperion, 1998. Print.

Secondary Sources

Andrews, Larry R. "Black Sisterhood in Gloria Naylor's Novels." *CLA Journal* 33 Sep. 1989: 1- 25.

Andrews, Williams L, Foster, Frances, Smith, and Harris, Trudier. *The Concise Oxford Companion to African American Literature*. New York: Oxford University Press. 2001.

Appiah and Gates (1993) In *Gloria Naylor: Critical Perspectives Past and Present*. Ed. Henry Louis Gates, Jr., and K.A. Appiah. New York: Amistad, 1993.

Arora, Neena (1999). "Gender Oppression in Gloria Naylor's *Women of Brewster Place* and *Linden Hills*," *The Indo–American Review* 7, Special Number on Afro – American Literature, ed. R.K. Dhawan (1999) 30.

Baker, Houston A. Jr. and Patricia Redmond. Afro-American Literary Study in the 1990s. Chicago and London: The University of Chicago Press, 1990.

Bala, Saroj (2002). "Kinship and Community in Gloria Naylor's *Linden Hills* and *Mama Day*," *Points of View*, vol. IX, no. 2 (winter 2002) 93.

Bell, Bernard W. The Contemporary African American Novel: *Its Folk Roots and Modern Literary Branches*. U.S.A: University of Massachusetts Press, 2004.

Berg, Christine G. (1999). "Light from a Hill of Carbon Paper Dolls": Gloria Naylor's "*Linden Hills*" and Dante's "*Inferno*"." *Modern Language Studies* (1999): 1-19.

Booker, M. Keith. Encyclopedia of Literature and Politics: *Censorship, Revolution, and Writing*. London: Greenwood Press, 2005.

Christian, Barbara. (106) "Naylor's Geography: Community, Class and Patriarchy in *The Women of Brewster Place* and *Linden Hills*."

Cleage, Pearl (1998). "Gloria Naylor," *Catalyst Summer* (1998): 57.

David, Brown and Clive, Webb. Race in the American South: From Slavery to Civil Rights. Edinburgh: Edinburgh University Press, 2007.

Davis, Charles T and Henry Louis Gates, Jr. (1985). "The Language of Slavery" *The Slave Narrative*. Eds. Oxford and New York: Oxford UP, 1985. xi–xxxiv. Print.

Dickson-Carr, Darryl. The Columbia Guide to Contemporary African American Fiction. New York: Columbia University Press, 2005.

Eko, Ebele. "Beyond the Myth of Confrontation: *A Comparative Study of African and African - American Female Protagonists*." *Ariel* 17 (1986): 139-52. Print.

Erickson, Peter. "Hard Work: Paule Marshall's Daughters." Callaloo 16.1 (1993):243.

Erickson, Peter. "*Shakespeare's Black?: the Role of Shakespeare in Naylor's Novels*."

Rewriting Shakespeare, Rewriting Ourselves. University of California, 1991. Rpt. *In Gloria Naylor: Critical Perspectives Past and Present*. New York: Amistad, 1993.

Erin, Weik. "Conjure in Mama Day." *African American Review* Dec. 1996: 1- 4. Print.

Flora, Joseph M and Mackethan, Lucinda H. *The Companion to Southern Literature: Themes, Genres, Places, People, Movements and Motifs*. Baton Rouge: Louisiana State University Press, 2002.

Fowler, Virginia C. Gloria Naylor: *In Search of Sanctuary*. New York: Twayne, 1996.

Freud, Sigmund. *"The interpretation of Dreams"* New York: Avon Books, 1998. Print

---. *"Dreams Psychology"* New York: Penguin, 1973. Print

---. *Introductory Lectures on Psychoanalysis.* The Pelican Freud Library. Volume 1. New York: Penguin, 1973. Print.

Francis, Ted. *Realism in the Novels of the Harlem Renaissance.* Lincoln: Writers Club Press, 2002.

Frye, Northrop (1957). *Anatomy of Criticism* (Princeton: Princeton UP, 1957) 40.

Gates, Henry Louis Jr. and K. A. Appiah (1993) *Past and Present.* Eds. New York: Amistad, 1993. 285-302. Print.

Goldstein, William (1983). *"A Talk with Gloria Naylor," Publishers Weekly* (Sep.9, 1983) 36.

Gottlieb, Annie (1982). *"The Women of Brewster Place," The New York Times Book Review.*

Graham, Maryemma and Ward, Jerry W. *The Cambridge History of African American Literature.* New York: Cambridge University Press, 2001.

Gray, Richard. *A History of American Literature.* Malden: Blackwell Publishing Ltd, 2004.

Hakutani, Yoshinobu. *Cross-Cultural Visions in African American Modernism: From Spatial Narrative to Jazz Haiku.* Columbus: The Ohio State University, 2006.

Harold, Bloom. *The Harlem Renaissance.* Philadelphia: Chelsea House Publishers, 2004.

Hayes, Elizabeth T. "Gloria Naylor's *Mama Day* as Magic Realism," *The Critical Response to Gloria Naylor.* Eds. Sharon Felton and Michelle C. Loris. Westport, Conn: Greenwood, 1977: 177-86. Print.

High, Peter B. An outline of American literature. New York: Longman Group, 1986.

Jacques, Geoffrey. A Change in the Weather: *Modernist Imagination African American Imaginary.* Amherst: University of Massachusetts Press, 2009.

James, R Giles., and Wanda H. *American Novelists* Since World War II. Vol. 173, Fifth Series. Detriot, Gale Group, 2002. Web 9 Feb. https://www.google.co.in/

Jarrett, Gene Andrew. *A companion to African American Literature.* Chichester, West Sussex, United Kingdom: Blackwell Companions to Literature and Culture, 2010.

Jones, Gayl. *Liberating Voices: Oral Tradition in African American Literature.* U.S.A: Harvard University Press, 1991.

Joseph, Peniel E. The Black Power Movement: *Rethinking the Civil Rights-Black Power Era.* New York: Routledge, 2006.

---. *Rethinking the Civil Rights-Black Power Era.* New York: Routledge, 2006.

Khaleghi, Mahboobeh. *"Female Leadership in Gloria Naylor's Novels: Blood mothers,Other mothers, and Community other mothers"* African American Review. J Soc.Sci. 2011: 131-138. Print.

Koolish, Lynda. *African American Writers: Portraits and Visions.* Jackson: University Press of Mississippi, 2004.

---. African American Writers: *Portraits and Visions.* Jackson: University Press of Mississippi, 2004.

Kubitschek, Missy Dehn. *"Subjugated Knowledge*: Toward a Feminist Exploration of Rape in Afro-American Fiction." *Black Feminist Criticism and Critical Theory.* Eds. Joe Weixlmann and Houston Baker. Greenwood, Florida: The Penkevill Publishing Company, 1988. 43-56. Print.

---. *Toni Morrison: A Critical Companion.* Westport: Greenwood P, 1998. Print.

Laurie, F. Leach. *Langston Hughes: A Biography.* London: Greenwood Press, 2004.

---. *Langston Hughes: A Biography.* London: Greenwood Press, 2004.

Matus, Jill L. (1990). "Dream, Deferral and Closure in *The Women of Brewster Place*," *Black American Literature Forum*, vol.24, no.1 (Spring 1990) 55.

Michelle, G Collins. "There Where We Are Not: The Magical Real in Beloved and Mama Day," Southern Review 1988: 680–685.

Print.

Mickey Pearlman and Katherine Usher Henderson, *"Interview"*, *Talks with America's Writing Women* (Kentucky: The University Press of Kentucky, 1990).

Miller, D. Quentin. The Routledge Introduction to African American Literature. New York: Taylor & Francis Group.

Mowat, Barbara A. and Paul Werstine (1994). Eds.. Shakespeare's *The Tempest* New York: Washington Square.

Naylor, Gloria. *Black Literature Criticism*. Vol.3 edited by James Draper. Detroit: Gale Research, 1992:1482 – 94. Print.

---. *Contemporary African American Novelists: A Bio – Bibliographical Critical Sourcebook*. Eds. Sarah Wheliss and Emmanuel S. Nelson. Westport, CT: Greenwood Press, 1999:366 – 76. Print.

Naylor, Gloria and Toni Morrison, "*A Conversation*," Southern Review 21.3 (1985): 579.

---. "*A Conversation*," Southern Review 21.3 (1985): 587.

---. "*A Conversation*." Southern Review, 1985: 596.

Neale, Hurston Zora *"Their Eyes Were Watching God"*, 1937.

Nelson, Emmanuel S. *Contemporary African American Novelists: a bio-bibliographical Critical Sourcebook*. U.S.A: Greenwood Press, 1999.

Newin, Keith. *The Oxford Handbook of American Literary Naturalism*. New York: Oxford University Press, 2011.

Oakes, Elizabeth H. *American Writers*. New York: Facts on File. Inc, 2004.

Patric, Henry. *A Review of Mama Day*. *Essence*. Aug. 2001: 62. Print.

Perry, Margaret. *A Bio-bibliography of Countée P. Cullen*. U.S.A: Greenwood Publishing Corporation.

Pam Cook, ed. "*History of Narrative Codes*." The Cinema Book. (1985. London; British Film, 1990.

Rangno, Erik V.P. *Contemporary American Literature*: 1945-Present. New York: DWJ Books LLC, 2006.

Ranveer, Kashinath (1995). *Black Feminist Consciousness,* (Jaipur: Print well Publishers, 1995) 120.

Ranveer, S, (1984). *"Black Women Novelists: New Generation Raises Provocative Issues,"* Ebony 40 (Nov.1984).

Reyes, Angelita. "Taking Flight and Taking Foot: From Margaret Garner to Beloved." *Mothering across Cultures: Postcolonial Representations.* Minneapolis, Minnesota: U Of Minnesota P, 2002. 33-77. Print.

Rowell, Charles H. "An Interview with Gloria Naylor." *Callaloo* 1997: 179-193. Print.

Smethurst, James. The African American Roots of Modernism: From Reconstruction to The Harlem Renaissance. U.S.A: The University of North Carolina Press, 2011.

Smith, Barbara (1977). "Toward a Black Feminist Criticism," *Conditions* (2 Oct. 1977): 32.

Smith, Jessie Carney. Encyclopaedia of African American Popular Culture. Colorado: Greenwood, 2011.

Smith, Rochelle and Jones, Sharon L. The Prentice Hall Anthology of African American Literature. U.S.A: Prentice Hall, 2000.

Sonal, Smrity and Rajni Singh (2018). *Violence, an Embedded Discourse of Multiculturalism in Gloria Naylor's The Women of Brewster Place IMPACT:* International Journal of Research in Humanities, Arts and Literature, Vol. 6, Issue 2, February 2018, 257-262.

Valli, K (2017). *Ramification of the Anguished African American Community in Gloria Naylor's Linden Hills.* Language in India, Vol. 17:12 December 2017.

Ward, Chatrine C. "Gloria Naylor's *Linden Hills*: A Modern Inferno." *Contemporary Literature* 28.1 (1987): 67-81.

---. "Gloria Naylor's *Linden Hills*: A Modern *Inferno.*" *Contemporary Literature* 28.1 (1987) 193.

Warren, Kenneth W. *What Was African American Literature?* London: Harvard University Press, 2001.

Whitt, -Margaret (1999). *Understanding Gloria Naylor* (Columbia: University of South Carolina Press, 1999) 55.

Whitt, Margaret Earley (1999). *Understanding Gloria Naylor* Columbia: South Carolina University Press, 1999. 73.

Williams, Sherley Anne (1985) *"Linden Hills* (1985)," *The New York Times Book Review* (June 1985) quoted. In Gloria Naylor, *Critical Perspectives Past and Present*, eds.

Henry Louise Gates, Jr. and K.A. Appiah (New York: Amistad, 1993) 10.

Wright, Elizabeth. *Psychoanalytic Criticism: A Reappraisal.* New York: Routledge, 1998. Print.

Wright, Richard. Literature of the Negro in the United States in Chapman's Black Voices. New York: New American Library, 1968. Print.

Worth, Richard. Slavery in the Americas: African Americans during Reconstruction. New York: Info Base publishing, 2006.